*Business Officers
In Higher Education:
A History of NACUBO*

Business Officers
In Higher Education:

A History of NACUBO

Neal O. Hines

National Association of College and University Business Officers

Washington, D.C.

Library of Congress Cataloging in Publication Data

Hines, Neal O.
   Business officers in higher education.

   Includes index.
   1. National Association of College and
University Business Officers—History.   I. Title.
LB2341.H53   378'.1'006073   82-3583
ISBN 0-915164-14-0   AACR2

Contents

Foreword

THIS HISTORY, BY NEAL O. HINES, documents many of the names and events that played a part in creating the organization known as the National Association of College and University Business Officers. It also traces the more recent activities that have led to the association's growth and success. No chronicle can properly account for the random juxtapositions of person, place, and time that affect history, and the story of NACUBO is no exception.

Though the forces for association and other major events were there all along, only business officers working together could effect change; it is no different today. The association takes great pride in its past, and has the resources to meet the management challenges of the future. Those resources are in its people, who have always "come through" when the circumstances demanded. One can wish no more for NACUBO than that the past is indeed prologue.

Those of us whose names appear below had the privilege of being president of the association. Most of this history is devoted to that period, which begins in 1962, but a knowledge of the years before that date is necessary for a fuller understanding of the association as it exists today. We are indebted to our many colleagues in that earlier period for having provided such a strong foundation, but especially to the presidents of the federation, which was established in 1951: Jamie R. Anthony, C. O. Emmerich, Irwin K. French, Nelson A. Wahlstrom, and Charles H. Wheeler III.

Kenneth D. Creighton	Thomas A. McGoey
Kenneth A. Dick	Robert W. Meyer
Merrill A. Ewing	Jesse B. Morgan
Robert B. Gilmore	Harold M. Myers
William T. Haywood	Orie E. Myers, Jr.
Mary M. Lai	Wilbur K. Pierpont
Anthony D. Lazzaro	James J. Ritterskamp, Jr.
Reuben H. Lorenz	Clarence Scheps
Roger D. Lowe	

Preface

THE NATIONAL ASSOCIATION of College and University Business Officers is an organization devoted to the cultivation of sound management in institutions of higher education in the United States.

The association reflects in 1982 almost three-quarters of a century of experience in its field. Not that it has existed so long in its present form: that form did not emerge until 1962, when there was created, at last, an organization identifiable by a new acronym, NACUBO. But the seeds of association were sown in 1909, and there followed after 1912 two successive periods of preliminary growth—two periods covering almost exactly fifty years—the first in which regional associations of business officers were founded and flourished in their special settings, and the second in which the regionals, joined by two other organizations with parallel professional objectives, came together in a loosely knit alliance called, somewhat awkwardly, the National Federation of College and University Business Officers Associations. From 1912 to 1962 the preparation was of that kind, and when the national association succeeded the federation, its base was in the strong regionals, and its inheritance included the professional interests and the traditions of service to higher education that had been building for so many years. With the opening of the association's national office in Washington, D.C. in 1967, the truly dynamic phase of service to higher education began. But the historic interests and traditions were there to build on.

What seems in 1982 most significant about NACUBO's development is the almost providential pace of it—the solid growth of half a century flowing finally into decades of professional activity in which the association's scope was expanded to meet with remarkable precision the needs of higher education in times of swift change. When the time came, the association grew at a phenomenal rate. The 1967 membership of 700 institutions had risen by 1982 to nearly 2,000. The costs of services and operations had moved from $102,000 at the opening of the national office to $2,730,000, with $304,000 of this in private and federal grants for the support of programs of national

1

impact. But the growth came because NACUBO proved flexible and imaginative, able to mobilize human resources, management experience, and ideas. NACUBO was prepared to grow. Business officers whose historic concerns were with accounting and financial reporting perfected their services in such fields while they worked on national committees dealing with new problems of costing, resource allocation, insurance and risk management, facilities planning, taxation, personnel management, and energy conservation. No business officer of the earlier breed—not even the business officer of 1962—could have foreseen the management demands that would come in the 1960s and 1970s with the Vietnam War, the new education and civil rights legislation, the energy shortages, unionization, and the rise of inflationary pressures. But NACUBO was ready to meet such times. It set up study programs supported by professional publications. It established new lines of communication to member institutions and to other associations and federal agencies. It prepared itself to serve higher education at the management level as the American Council on Education served at the level of policy. NACUBO had found its place.

This narrative traces NACUBO's growth from the tentative beginnings, but emphasis is on the association years, particularly the years after 1967 when NACUBO went to Washington, with only enough of the background to make proper connections with the origins. For the early history has been done. The history through the federation period was prepared two decades ago by a man who had been a well-known participant in professional affairs. That historian was Clifton C. DeLong, former bursar of the University of Illinois. Business officers remain in his debt.

DeLong was familiar with professional efforts from prefederation days. In the 1930s he had served under Lloyd Morey, comptroller and later president of the University of Illinois, who already had published a pioneering text, *University and College Accounting,* and who had headed an American Council on Education National Committee on Standard Reports for Institutions of Higher Education. DeLong took part in early post-World War II conferences on the principles of cost reimbursement under federal grants and contracts. When the regional associations were moving into federation, DeLong was there—a representative of his own regional association to the planning meetings of 1950, host to the Chicago meetings of 1951 at which the federation was created, chairman of the program committee for the federation's first national assembly at Estes Park in 1955, and the principal agent of the federation when the organization was incorporated in Illinois in 1956. Writing that first history, DeLong was working with memories as well as with records, and his account, *A History of the National Federation of College and University Business Officers Associations,* was published with national association support just as the new organization was preparing to hold its first national meeting in Pittsburgh in July 1963. A decade later DeLong drafted a history of the association to 1970. This manuscript, completed in 1972 and reproduced in limited numbers, remains in association archives, a resource available to all who would examine the story of that later period. For his contributions to the professional record, DeLong was honored by NACUBO at its annual meeting in Denver in 1972.

It is too much to expect that this history can acknowledge, fully and fairly, the contributions of the many business officers who have served the association over the years. They number in the hundreds. A smaller number, but still many—and even some persons outside the association—were involved in some way in the compilation and review of this record, among them current and former officers, directors, and committee members who read all or parts of the manuscript. On the roster of those who gave such help are the names of James W. Bryant, Ernest M. Conrad, Kenneth D. Creighton, Charles G. Dobbins, William T. Haywood, J. Leslie Hicks, Jr., Robert F. Kerley, Anthony D. Lazzaro, Reuben H. Lorenz, Roger D. Lowe, Thomas A. McGoey, Harold M. Myers, Wilbur K. Pierpont, W. Harold Read, Clarence Scheps, Fred S. Vorsanger, and Howard P. Wile. All of these have the association's thanks, as do D. Francis Finn and members of the national staff, whose notes and suggestions were of great value, and particularly Abbott Wainwright, who coordinated and supervised the project from the beginning.

To one other contributor generous acknowledgment is due. Kenneth A. Dick was vice president for business and finance at the University of Idaho for many years, an active leader of the Western Association, a participant in the evolution of the national federation, and a consistent spokesman for the movement that eventually produced NACUBO. After the national association had come into existence, Dick was its president from 1963 to 1965. He was the first executive vice president when the national office was opened in 1967, serving there until his retirement in 1969. To the preparation of this history Dick contributed a set of notes covering his recollections and impressions of events within his experience, all of great help in the effort to trace with understanding the course of NACUBO's growth.

3

The story is of the development of a single association within the body of American higher education. The story's larger interest, if any, will depend on the accuracy with which it reflects, from a special point of view, the evolutions in higher education itself. The hope, at least, is that the larger interest is present. May it be so.

1909-1949: To Build a Base

IN NOVEMBER 1909 the principal business officers of six Midwest state institutions—the Universities of Michigan, Wisconsin, Illinois and Missouri, and the Ohio State University and Iowa State College—met on the campus of a privately supported institution, Northwestern University, at Evanston, Illinois, to talk about accounting and financial reporting. The meeting probably was the first of its kind. It took place, in any event, in a time of interesting stirrings.

There had arrived on the scene a new force in American higher education. This was the Carnegie Foundation for the Advancement of Teaching, created earlier in the decade by Andrew Carnegie and headed, as president, by Henry S. Pritchett, who had been brought by Carnegie from the Massachusetts Institute of Technology. Pritchett had attempted certain broad analyses of the body of higher education, first trying to identify institutions by type, then to establish criteria for measuring "efficiency" in their management. Soon he had turned to financial reporting, searching for uniformity of format; to the gathering of information he had assigned his foundation auditor, Harvey S. Chase, a Boston CPA whose accounting firm was conducting, by 1909, surveys of institutional practice. The Chase firm also had, in fact, installed a new system of accounting at Northwestern, and when the business officers met at Evanston that November, Chase was present to explain the Northwestern system.

The Evanston meeting was a small one, but it reflected a new interest in cooperative action almost certainly stimulated by the Carnegie studies. Business officers were comparing notes. Carl E. Steeb of Ohio State had visited neighboring institutions that autumn, and Shirley W. Smith of Michigan had visited others in the Midwest and East. They had sensed a mood, and the Northwestern meeting confirmed it. Before the business officers left Evanston, they adopted a resolution that soon would be circulated among other institutions. The resolution: ". . .We would favor the formation of an association of the officers in charge of the business administration of the state colleges and universities of the Middle West," with annual meetings to discuss "unification of accounting, uniformity of annual reports, purchasing system, inventory system, etc."

In 1909 association had been expressed as a goal—association of state institutions, and only in the Midwest, at least for a start. The proposal thus was limited, and limited further by the phrasing of the resolution which made the idea "subject to the approval of the governing bodies" of the prospective members. But the approvals came during what proved to be two years of organizational spadework, and early in 1912 an association of business officers finally had been created.[1]

The association of 1912 was a seed barely germinating. Just fourteen persons were present at what was the first recorded meeting, held January 12 and 13 of that year in the Auditorium Hotel in Chicago. But to the nucleus of 1909 had been drawn recruits from Indiana University, the Universities of Minnesota and Kansas, and what were then the Kansas State and Michigan Agricultural Colleges. (Also attending was Clyde Furst, secretary of the Carnegie Foundation.) There had been intermediate developments. In August 1910 certain "secretaries and accountants," as the recorder described them, had attended a Detroit meeting called to discuss a proposed new national association of registrars and business officers of state universities, but the business officers had withdrawn, considering their interests somewhat apart from those of the registrars. Later, at a meeting known thereafter as "the lost meeting" because no minutes ever were found, the "secretaries and accountants" had elected Michigan's Shirley Smith as their leader, and Smith had set about getting an association organized. So by 1912 an association existed, regional in scope. The name defined it. It was the Association of Business Officers of the State Universities and Colleges of the Middle West.[2]

What, in the long view, were the meanings of this? At the simplest level, the business officers of a cluster of Midwest public universities and colleges—nudged, doubtless, by the Carnegie inquiries—had moved for the first time into a realm of mutual consultation and action on financial management questions important to their institutions. Of far broader significance was the fact that, of all who held administrative responsibilities in higher education, business officers were among the first to organize for such service.

American higher education in 1912 was in the twilight of an era that would end with World War I. Institutions of the highest quality were abundant, institutions which already had established the standards for education in the humanities, the sciences, and the professions; their diversity had long been recognized as a strength. But the scale needs to be recalled. Even the largest institutions were small by later measurements, whether in enrollment, faculty, plant, or administrative capacity. The nation's population was at 92 million—it was in 1912 that New Mexico and Arizona were admitted as the forty-seventh and forty-eighth states—and only a fraction of the young people of college age were enrolling for college training. At the leadership level, higher education had presidents and educators of stature and vision, persons representing the best traditions of education in a free society; but common action or consultation was rather more in the style of professional mingling and personal communication than in mobilization for determination of broad policy, much less national policy. The presidents of private institutions tended their loyal flocks, the presidents of public institutions their legislatures and constituencies. A federal education office had been set up in 1867 in the Department of the Interior, but not until 1913 did the federal government begin to devote comprehensive attention to surveys of higher education practices and problems. And not until after World War I would there be an American Council on Education to support the institutions' own studies of issues before them.

As for university business procedures in 1912, they were, obviously, still formative. Public institutions for years had been publishing annual statements of receipts and disbursements, but many of these reports, as Pritchett had found, were mere listings of vouchers, meaningless as reflections of institutional operations, objectives, or priorities. The mass of institutions simply made no public accounting at all. The titles of business officers—bursar, treasurer, secretary, even comptroller—were derived from traditional concepts of the officers' supporting roles. One of the first "business managers" had appeared in the 1890s at the University of Chicago, where John D. Rockefeller was experimenting with management ideas in the university he had so heavily endowed. Chicago also had one of the first staff auditors, who was, fortunately for the profession, Trevor Arnett, who would be heard from later. Rockefeller had asked Chicago administrators for annual reports on their plans and estimates of their financial needs, but this early step toward institutional budgeting was a development then almost universally ignored. Rockefeller was experimenting, and the Rockefeller Foundation would become in time a major supporter of studies of management and finance, but it was the Carnegie inquiries that signaled most clearly what was coming. When the foundation published in 1910 the results of Harvey Chase's work, "Standard Forms for Financial Reports of Colleges, Universities, and Technical

Schools," it had completed successfully the first broad survey of institutional practices and had created, with the help of the universities, the first exploratory models in the field of financial reporting.[3]

But World War I was coming, altering many things. The Association of Business Officers of the State Universities and Colleges of the Middle West held its meetings in that period—in the last years of peace, in the years when war in Europe came to stalemate on the western front, and in 1917 and 1918 when students were leaving college campuses to go to France with the American Expeditionary Forces and the campuses themselves were becoming centers of wartime training. Whatever else university management was then, it was emergency management of an unprecedented kind. As would happen again a generation later, war changed American education and challenged its management. After the war—only then—the search for more comprehensive approaches could begin.

The association of Midwest state universities could not, of course, remain as it had begun—exclusively Midwest and exclusively state. By 1919, when private institutions also were represented in the membership, the "State" was dropped. The next year, because institutions outside the Midwest were rallying, the "Middle West" was discarded, and the organization became simply the Association of University and College Business Officers. But a movement toward separate organization was underway, with the locus in the East, where private institutions were strong. From preliminary organizational meetings in October and November, 1920—the first at the University of Pennsylvania, the second at Johns Hopkins—there emerged a second association, the Association of University and College Business Officers of the Eastern States. Leaders in this organization were F. H. Eckels of the University of Pittsburgh and W. O. Miller of Pennsylvania; but the first president was C. S. Danielson of Columbia, with Eckels the permanent secretary. The Midwest seedling of 1912 had put out new roots, but there were two independent associations now, not just a larger one. A pattern was being established that would be characteristic of the mobilization of business officers as professionals.[4]

What had happened may seem, decades later, an anomaly. For while the business officers, having been among the first to organize, were organizing regionally, two groups of officers whose responsibilities were in the business field were organizing nationally. As early as 1914, the directors of physical plant had formed a national Association of Superintendents of Buildings and Grounds. And by 1921 the college and university purchasing agents had done the same, creating at a meeting in Indianapolis a new Educational Buyers Association, a national organization with J. C. Christensen of Michigan its first president. The time would come, although not soon, when the Educational Buyers Association—by then the National Association of Educational Buyers (NAEB)—would join business officers in the first alliance national in scope.[5]

The decade of the 1920s—the decade before the Great Depression set in—seems after half a century a time of earnest but intermittent striving toward the goals that had been glimpsed before the late war: better management, improved "efficiency" in operations, far greater uniformity in accounting and reporting, a sounder grasp of costing. In the records of the associations and of national committees were appearing the names of persons who, through their own writings or as participants in national studies, would become the leaders of growth toward professionalism. Lloyd Morey, of the University of Illinois—who would become in time his university's president—had been attending Midwest meetings since 1916. Trevor Arnett had been attending since 1918, when Chicago became one of the private institutions joining the Midwest group, and by 1921 Arnett had published his *College and University Finance,* a pioneering contribution to the literature. As the 1930s followed the 1920s, there came others whose names would be associated with an expanding professional activity, among them E. S. Erwin of Stanford; Thad Hungate of Teachers College, Columbia; J. Harvey Cain of the Catholic University of America; Thomas E. Blackwell of Washington University; George E. Van Dyke, a student of Morey and Arnett, later associated with major professional editorial projects; Gail A Mills, long at Princeton; and Michigan's Christensen who, having helped launch the Educational Buyers Association, would move to new responsibilities But in those decades it was the American Council on Education, with support from the Carnegie and Rockefeller Foundations, that became the rallying point for business officers working at the national level on issues of management principle and practice.

The American Council, established in 1918-19, had created in 1921, with Carnegie help, an Educational Finance Inquiry Commission which produced in 1925 a thirteen-volume report. Soon the U.S. Office of Education, which by then was conducting surveys of costs in higher education, was taking the lead in pressing for standardization in accounting and reporting. The response came again from the American Council, which organized in 1930 a National Committee on Standard Reports for Institutions of Higher Education, a committee headed by Morey and thereafter known, naturally, as the "Morey committee." Morey that year had published his own early text, *University and College Accounting,* but as committee chairman he appointed

9

Hungate of Columbia to make a comparative study of the financial statements of about a hundred institutions; and when those materials had been digested, the final report of the committee, *Financial Reports for Colleges and Universities,* was published in 1935 by the University of Chicago Press. By that time the American Council, with financing by Carnegie and help from business officers, was developing its Financial Advisory Service, a consultative and reference center headed first by Van Dyke, then by Cain. In a movement of such deep concern to them, business officers were moving to center stage. They had in the interim completed a circle of regional professional associations and were about to collaborate, under the auspices of the American Council, in an historic effort to bring together the essential guidelines for higher education administration.[6]

Organizations of business officers in the South and West had not followed immediately those in the Midwest and East. Not until 1928 was a Southern Association created—at a meeting in Atlanta, with G. H. Mew of Emory University as its first president. In the West the procedure was even more deliberate. Business officers there had been talking for years about organizing—even as early as 1920, apparently—but it was in 1936 that a Western Association finally was formed by representatives of thirty-four institutions (Lloyd Morey had been helpful in this, too), with Stanford's E. S. Erwin as president, H. A. Bork of the Oregon State System of Higher Education, vice president, and H. H. Benedict of the University of California, secretary-treasurer. In neither the South nor the West, however, had there been lack of interest or participation in the activities going forward. Business officers of many institutions simply had taken memberships in the established associations and were contributing to the support of professional programs—one of these being Erwin, who had been a member of the editorial group working with the Morey committee after 1930. But with four regional associations now in place, and before there was any perceptible feeling for possible national affiliation, business officers were ready to move together in support of a national project of landmark significance—the development of a definitive guide touching all areas of college and university business administration.[7]

For years the pressures for standard or generally acceptable formats and procedures had been rising. The technical discussions at regional meetings invariably touched the issues. With its *Financial Reports,* the Morey committee had produced a guide of unquestioned authority, and the American Council's Financial Advisory Service was publishing pamphlets (ultimately twenty-one of these) covering the principal management topics. But the success of these efforts whetted appetites for a publication of equal authority but broader in range. The Midwest business officers discussed the idea at their 1937 meeting. The following year, representatives of the four regional associations, meeting in Pittsburgh, established a National Committee on the Preparation of a Manual on College and University Business Administration. The chairman was J. C. Christensen. A "manual committee" had been born, and it would produce—after another world war and a passage of years—that most definitive and widely accepted guide, *College and University Business Administration* ("Volumes I and II").[8]

There came in that time, too, a professional development of another kind but of singular symbolism. Business officers of four black institutions—Howard University, Tuskegee and Hampton Institutes, and Virginia State College—met at Howard in April 1939 to organize an Association of Business Officers in Schools for Negroes.* The new association would eventually become the American Association, not a regional but considered a part of the regional association circle. But not for more than a quarter of a century—not until after it had celebrated its twenty-fifth anniversary in 1964, and not until there was a national association—would its member institutions (by then about forty of what still were called the "predominantly Negro institutions") stand with others in the professional alignment.[9]

By 1939 war was nearing in Europe. But just before the world changed again, the business officers engaged in a brief flurry of talks about forming a national alliance.

It was in the central group—still the Association of University and College Business Officers—that the idea was approached in its 1939 meeting.** The association adopted a resolution urging that "the various regional and functional groups" send representatives to a meeting "to explore the possibility of some form of federation and of a more integrated program for the business management of higher education." Two meetings actually were held, one in 1939, another in 1940.

---

*The record shows that the Central Association was the first to accept membership of Negro institutions. Fisk University, represented by a white business officer, was accepted in 1929. In the same year, the Eastern Association accepted membership from Hampton Institute, whose business officer was also white. But in the 1930s no association would accept Negro colleges with Negro business officers. It became evident in the late 1930s that a new organization would have to be formed with the special mission of securing the benefits of group efforts and of making a concerted attack on those problems aggravated by segregation policies.[10]

** The Midwest "Association of University and College Business Officers" became the Central Association only in 1940, and it would remain until 1946 an association of "University and College" business officers. Not until 1939 had the "Association of University and College Business Officers of the Eastern States" become, at last, simply the Eastern Association of College and University Business Officers. Even such adjustments in nomenclature had come slowly.

11

The four regionals sent delegates, and so did the Educational Buyers Association, the Association of Superintendents of Buildings and Grounds, and the Financial Advisory Service of the American Council. The first meeting suggested "some form of group planning." But nothing came of this. What came was World War II.[11]

To an extent undreamed of in 1917-18, the college and university campuses were converted after 1941 to wartime training and, this time, to war-related research. The explosion of research on the campuses was a new element, and management involved adjustment to federal procurement requirements and contract reimbursement policies. But everything was changed for the duration—regular enrollments at minimums, many faculty members and administrators serving in the armed forces, management subject to change, crisis, or improvisation. Even so—and remarkably—business officers who had rejected national federation in 1939 kept alive in the war years that national effort to develop a comprehensive guide to higher education administration.

Christensen's manual committee was in being, but financial support was essential. Again, major help came from the Carnegie Foundation. Carnegie grants to the American Council in 1942 and 1943 put the "manual" project in motion, and additional contributions were made by the regional associations and the Association of Business Officers in Schools for Negroes. When the war finally was over, Blackwell became editor in 1946, and by that time the effort was under the general leadership of Arthur W. Peterson of the University of Wisconsin, who headed the executive committee as the American Council's representative. Peterson's associates were Morey, Erwin, L. H. Foster, Jr. of Tuskegee, A. M. Graham of Winthrop College, and A. S. Johnson of Rutgers.[12]

Not for half a dozen years would the first fruit of the "manual" project appear, that long-awaited Volume I of *College and University Business Administration,* published by the American Council on Education. But it would have seemed that a national effort so dependent on business officer experience would suggest a clear need for business officer participation in this and other projects from or through an identifiable national base. It was not until the end of the 1940s, however—five years after World War II and decades after the beginnings in the Midwest—that business officers were ready to bring their separate associations into national federation.

2

1950-1962: The Path to Association

ORGANIZATION BY REGION and by region alone (the organization by
black business officers implicitly recognized as a regional development) was a form with which business officers of most colleges and
universities had seemed content until World War II. Then and thereafter, feelings began to change. But change came slowly, and it was not
until 1950 that a national structure evolved. It is risky to try to re-
construct attitudes, but it may be appropriate to look more closely at
the background against which organizational developments took the
course they did.

What the business officers' regional association activities had culti-
vated over the years were feelings of community of the closest kind.
As professionals (and their views of their own professionalism remained somewhat ambivalent), business officers had functioned at
two levels, the national and the local. Selected business officers from
all regions had taken part in those programs of national sweep, such
as the American Council's committee mobilization and the preparation of *Financial Reports;* these efforts and the results were all duly
reported and discussed at the regional associations' annual meetings.
Yet to the business officer facing the daily demands at the institution,
the high-level searches for management principle could not but have
seemed remote. The business officer of the typical institution—typically small, whether public or private—had been engaged in professional growth closer to home, finding counsel where available. For
years this had been the case. In the 1930s, the business officer and the
institution lived in the trenches of the Great Depression, expenses cut
to the bone. A travel budget designed primarily to meet academic
requirements rarely had room for the professional needs of the person who managed the funds. In the years when most long-distance
travel was by rail, a business officer's trip to a national meeting usually
would have seemed prohibitively expensive—in travel costs, in time
away from the desk—to all but the few. To the "average" business
officer, the regional meeting was the only possible professional contact, and one might use one's own automobile, one's own funds, and
part of one's vacation time to get there. (Association dues were kept
low, and sometimes even the expenses of officers and directors were

not reimbursed.) The regional associations had come along in their own ways and times, but each had grown strong in such loyalty and shared purpose. Workshops were regional. Communication was regional, usually by an occasional newsletter. And in the publication of its annual proceedings, each association had created a literature of its own, a literature of both immediate usefulness and historical value because it was, simply, regional. That was the background. How, or in what form, could change appear?[1]

Every development of the World War II decade, from the war itself to the era of postwar readjustment, had underscored the need for creative responses in fields with which the university business officer was most familiar. The research institutions of classic mold had been recognized during the war as sources of national strength, and many were continuing to house or manage research laboratories of great size and sophistication, each surrounded by new problems of funding, staffing, university-government relationships, and cost reimbursement. But every higher education institution had been affected in some new way. The campuses were flooded by veterans seeking training under the GI Bill, and this while most institutions were having to catch up with construction, maintenance, or staffing put aside during the war years. Higher education was an element of national policy, and the pressures on financial management had risen accordingly. The time had come, surely, for such management to assert itself—to represent the institutions, and preferably through mechanisms that could achieve some degree of national consensus.

But for the business officers, the 1946-49 period had been one of movement toward a decision which even then seemed to the leaders strangely slow in coming. At the national level, work had continued on Volume I of *College and University Business Administration,* Peterson and Blackwell at the center, but the "manual" impulse was prewar in origin, and the text could only be shaped as necessary to accommodate the new realities of the postwar era. What was perhaps most telling was that, while the regional associations had been talking about federation (the Southern and Eastern associations adopted resolutions in 1948), events had threatened to overtake them. As early as 1946, Robert B. Stewart of Purdue, who had been active during the war on questions related to federally sponsored research, had organized a committee of business officers from various research institutions to discuss with War and Navy Department representatives the principles governing reimbursement of costs including "overhead." With no central organization to turn to, Stewart simply had drawn together an ad hoc team of experienced administrators, and from conferences in Chicago with

14

government representatives had come by 1947 what was called the "blue book," its formal title, "Principles for Determination of Costs Under Government Research and Development Contracts with Educational Institutions." Among business officers who had joined Stewart in that effort were several whose leadership would be important in the future, among them William T. Middlebrook and Laurence R. Lunden of Minnesota, Wilbur K. Pierpont of Michigan, Morey and C. C. DeLong of Illinois, and, of course, Peterson and Blackwell.* By so much, business officers without a national organization behind them had moved forthrightly into a field that would be a preoccupation for decades after national organization was achieved. But it was noteworthy, too, that other business-related organizations had been forming. In 1946, the personnel officers had created the College and University Personnel Association, and by 1949 there was a Campus Safety Association and an Association of College and University Housing Officers. Still, at the end of the 1940s, the business officers were regional.[2]

What happened at that turning point was predictable and understandable. The business officers determined to form a federation of the kind they had been discussing since the late 1930s. No national headquarters was yet contemplated, but there would be national officers and committees, and the regional associations would be the building blocks for a professional structure that could project at the national level the management ideas or proposals percolating below. What was unpredictable was the way it occurred. It is an interesting part of the professional lore that even that first step into the realm of national action is attributable in large measure to the effect of an editorial in a relatively new magazine that had become the unofficial "journal" of the business officers.

The magazine was *College and University Business,* founded in 1946 by the Nation's Schools Publishing Co., a wholly owned subsidiary of the Modern Hospital Publishing Co. of Chicago, but soon a publication of McGraw-Hill. Its managing editor was Harold W. Herman, an imaginative and self-motivated young man who, in four years, by conscientious coverage of regional association activities and by encouraging contributions of articles by business officers, had won for himself and his magazine the respect and confidence of the profes-

---

*Other participants in the 1946 university-government talks were W. R. Stott, Caltech; Joseph Campbell, Columbia; G. A. Rosselot, Georgia Tech; H. S. Baker, Johns Hopkins; J. R. Killian, Jr., M.I.T.; H. L. Wells and J. M. Brooks, Northwestern; G. A. Mills, Princeton; W. B. Harrell and H. C. Daines, Chicago; R. S. Thompson, Rochester; and C. D. Simmons, Texas. (DeLong, *Federation,* p. 37)

15

sionals. The magazine had no official status, but major articles were subject to review by an editorial advisory board composed of leading business officers. An editorial in *College and University Business* thus commanded attention. It was in an editorial of July 1950 that Herman—taking a cue from a recent move within the Central Association and quoting at length from comments by Lloyd Morey—said, "It's time that the movement came of age."

The Central Association, meeting that spring in Urbana, Illinois, had authorized its executive committee to negotiate with representatives of other associations, including the National Association of Educational Buyers, for formation of a "national organization" that would hold meetings "at least once every three years." The Herman editorial was geared to the recent Central action, and it quoted Morey; but it opened with an exceedingly pointed paragraph that must have had the knowledge of the business officer leadership at large:

> "Observers of the higher education field have been at a loss to understand why business managers of colleges and universities have never organized on a national basis. The business managers seem to have taken a stubborn delight in maintaining their provincial isolation from their colleagues in other parts of the country."

Herman was blunt, but the burden of the argument for national unity lay in the comments by Morey:

> "The development of our professional organization has differed from that of other administrative and academic groups in that it has been regional rather than national.
> "This has both advantages and disadvantages. One advantage is closer proximity of meetings to a larger proportion of membership, with less cost of transportation and probably greater attendance. . . .The disadvantages are that each organization tends to be more provincial in character, that experiences are not shared or enjoyed as widely . . . and that the profession lacks a solid and united front on problems that are of general and nationwide concern. The last named point was particularly evident during the recent war, and continues to be important in current government relationships.
> "I list as one of my major disappointments the inability of our business officer organizations to get together on a permanent basis."

To see the Herman editorial as a catalyst, it is necessary to note only the rapidity of the ensuing events. In August 1950—a month after the editorial appeared—a general letter suggesting a meeting was sent to the other business officer associations by Jamie R. Anthony of the Georgia Institute of Technology, president of the Southern Association. By the end of the month, a meeting had been scheduled at the University of Illinois Illini Center in the LaSalle Hotel in Chicago, the facility offered by DeLong, secretary of the Central Association. When association representatives came together on September 11 and 12, 1950, they resolved to establish, subject to ratification by the various memberships, a National Federation of College and University Business Officers Associations. Soon the federation existed in fact. Jamie Anthony was its president.[3]

The new organization was something of a conglomerate, the four regional associations joined by the American Association (until that year the Association of Business Officers in Schools for Negroes) and the National Association of Educational Buyers, within which there had been for years an extensive overlapping of business officer membership.* With Anthony as president were James M. Miller of the University of California, vice president, and Irwin K. French of Middlebury College, secretary-treasurer. Directors were from the constituent groups: the American Association was represented by Foster of Tuskegee; the Central by DeLong, by John K. Selleck, Nebraska, and by Bert C. Ahrens of the NAEB; the Eastern by French and by H. R. Patton, Carnegie Tech; the Southern by Anthony and by Gerald D. Henderson, Vanderbilt; the Western by Miller; and the NAEB itself by the Rev. J. Leo Sullivan, College of the Holy Cross.

Federation had provided, at last, a professional center, even if the center had as yet no fixed address. At the preliminary meeting of 1950, there had been not only discussion of structure—Selleck had headed the Committee on Organization—but of professional objectives: one "to develop and improve principles and practices of educational business administration," another "to foster and maintain . . . professional ideals and standards." The future objectives had been cast rather more specifically: to assure that "points of view . . . on matters of national interest" were available to federal agencies, and "to give nationwide . . . scope to the work of developing and improving principles and practices" of financial administration. When the bylaws of the new federation were approved on June 25, 1951, an organization was there for all to see. The purposes were

---

*In 1961 Lloyd Morey recalled, in a talk at the Central Association meeting, that there had existed until the mid-1930s a commercially published magazine, the *Educational Business Manager and Buyer,* founded a decade earlier to serve the purchasing agents but soon widened in content to attract business officer readership. The publication had no official connection with the NAEB, but its presence may have helped cement the relationship between the buyers and the business officers.

17

reaffirmed. A board of directors composed of two members from each association would elect officers at meetings to be held not later than June 30 of each year. There would be a permanent National Federation Committee, a standing committee, and other committees as events required. It was time, now, for congratulation and for more planning.

It was evident in 1950-51 that federation had come in the nick of time. Peterson, Blackwell, and the volunteer "manual committee" laborers were completing their work on Volume I of *College and University Business Administration* (the federation board praised the effort), and the American Council would be publishing it in 1952. But there also was now a national sponsorship for consultations of the kind initiated by Robert Stewart in 1946. The "blue book" of 1947 had been incorporated into Chapter XV of the *Armed Services Procurement Regulation,* but the contract research issues were still requiring consistent attention, and since 1948 an interassociation committee composed of representatives of the regionals and functioning under the chairmanship of Middlebrook of Minnesota had been representing the universities in contacts with the Department of Defense, the Veterans Administration, the Public Health Service, and the Atomic Energy Commission, each an agency that was tending to establish particularized requirements with respect to research sponsorship and reimbursement.* Middlebrook's committee did not at once become a committee of the federation—that would happen in 1954—but from the moment the federation was established, Middlebrook regularly reported to the directors and enjoyed the support of a national organization.

However the national federation is viewed historically, its inherent weaknesses as a professional force are apparent. The six federated groups—the four regionals, the American Association, and the NAEB—represented a combined membership of about 600 institutions. Management was by a board (three members from each association after 1953) that met annually. There was no national office, that idea invariably rejected because of cost, and there were no provisions for regular communication, for periodic meetings of the membership,

---

*Members of the original interassociation committee were: *American Association,* J. B. Clarke of Howard; *Central Association,* Middlebrook, Louis V. Phelps of Grinnell, and Harry L. Wells of Northwestern; *Eastern Association,* F. Morris Cochran of Brown, J. Harvey Cain, and Henry W. Herzog of George Washington; *Southern Association,* W. T. Ingram of Alabama Polytechnic, Jamie Anthony, and Gerald Henderson; *Western Association,* James Corley of California and H. A. Bork of Oregon State System.

or for the necessary intensive consultations outside the normal range of what was, after 1954, the national federation's Committee on Governmental Relations. Management was remote from membership, and without general communication or membership meetings, it was impossible to achieve general consensus on anything.*

The issue was not simply one of small institutions versus large, although such an element was present. Actually, three kinds of thinking were detectable. The "big" institutions were those more accurately identified as the graduate and research institutions heavily involved in federally sponsored programs. To them it was immediately and explicitly important to meet the federal agencies face to face on questions of principle in management and reimbursement. Robert Stewart's committee had begun this, William Middlebrook's had continued the effort, and by 1958 the Bureau of the Budget would be publishing, as successor to the "blue book," BOB Circular A-21 in which statements of cost principles were refined. But to other institutions, constituting the bulk of the federation membership—typically the four-year liberal arts institution or the state college—such requirements had almost no meaning. They could ill afford federation membership if it imposed larger costs. They could see no reason to support national activities, particularly a national office and staff, that could not be justified as of some practical benefit to them. On neither of these sides—the research institution on one, the "small" college on the other—was there yet a clear view of what might be achieved in the way of pure professional work for the profession's sake. Among the leaders were more than a few who did have this view, however, and they represented the third kind of thinking—at the center the hope that business officers, growing together in workshops, exchanges of information, research on institutional problems, and professional publication, would win their proper places at the highest levels of higher education policy making. But they were not there yet. For national meetings the national agenda had to be designed. Communication required staff work. Publication demanded research. Some sense of national purpose—a national program, however modest— was essential.

The program that took shape between 1953 and 1960 contained, but in embryo, each of the activities properly associated with profes-

---

*A demonstration of the weakness came early. At its meeting of 1952, the federation board adopted a resolution expressing unqualified endorsement of the "Teague bill," a measure affecting benefits for veterans, and copies were duly dispatched to members of Congress and others. Immediately there followed protests by a number of federation institutions, which held that the board could not speak for all.

sional growth—national meetings, publication, research, more consistent communication, consultative activities, and tightened contact with other groups in higher education, particularly the American Council. Nothing came rapidly, but the period was a necessary warm-up, a period in which business officers and new leaders gained experience in thinking nationally, in which the idea of national association flowered, and in which there appeared the first really serious talk of establishing a national office.

The federation's national meetings were not annual or even biennial. They were (since the federation board and regional associations were meeting annually) quinquennial—and called "quinquennial assemblies"—the first in 1955, at Estes Park, Colorado, and the second in 1960, at French Lick, Indiana. Peculiar as the five-year concept may appear to later generations, the records of each assembly show that the programs were strong, the attendance surprisingly wide. Each meeting generated a participatory excitement that must have provided an antidote to whatever "provincialism" had been detected. And, after 1955, certain new leaders were being identified, and the federation was involved in projects that were clearly professional.

Jamie Anthony had served as president until 1953 when he was succeeded by Irwin French, with Gerald Henderson of Vanderbilt the vice president, and the secretary-treasurer Nelson A. Wahlstrom of the University of Washington. By 1955 Wahlstrom was president, and he was followed in 1957 by C. O. Emmerich of Emory University, and in 1959 by Charles H. Wheeler III of the University of Richmond. In the lists of federation board members were the names of others who would have roles of some importance after association arrived—from the American Association, James W. Bryant, then of Texas College, Harold K. Logan, then of Wiley, and B. A. Little of Southern University; from the Central Association, Wilbur Pierpont; from the Eastern, Kurt M. Hertzfeld, then of the University of Rochester, and Edward K. Cratsley of Swarthmore; from the Southern, Clarence Scheps of Tulane; and from the Western, George W. Green of Caltech, Kenneth A. Dick of the University of Idaho, and Ernest M. Conrad of the University of Washington. A capacity for continuity was being established.

By the time Wahlstrom became president of the federation, the American Council was publishing Volume II of *College and University Business Administration,* which meant that the federation could take pride in the decade of volunteer work that business officers had contributed to that pioneering program. A. W. Peterson had continued as chairman of the executive committee, which included, again, E. S. Erwin and L. H. Foster, Jr., but with three new members, William Middlebrook, John F. Meck of Dartmouth, and Clarence Scheps, the final editorial committee including Peterson, Middlebrook, and George Van Dyke, then assistant comptroller of the Rockefeller Foundation. The experience had proved something that had become more apparent all along—that both the American Council and the federation would benefit from a continuing relationship. Thus in 1956, a year after Volume II appeared, Wahlstrom appointed a special committee of six—Emmerich, French, Pierpont, Miller, Wheeler, and H. L. Doten of Maine—to explore new American Council-National Federation service roles; and when the committee was reconstituted the following year, the new chairman was Kurt Hertzfeld, who became the federation delegate to council meetings. In the meantime two serious professional efforts were in process—one a study of income and expenditures of sixty privately supported liberal arts colleges, the other an effort to develop a National Federation Consulting Service.[4]

The income-expenditure study had been conceived in 1954, its object to assemble from colleges of similar character data on their "fixed" and administrative costs as a step toward control. The idea was new, interesting, and potentially valuable. The data were published, with support from the Fund for the Advancement of Education, as *A Study of Income and Expenditures in Sixty Colleges—Year 1953-54*. The subject colleges were from the federation associations, and their business officers were intimately associated with planning and reporting. By 1958, because comparative data were needed, the study was repeated—again with the help of the colleges and the support of the fund—the results published this time as *The Sixty College Study—A Second Look*. And this time the project was conducted under the auspices of the National Federation Consulting Service, of which Irwin French was executive director.[5]

The sixty-college project was a solid effort—a solid demonstration, too, of what might be attempted professionally on a national basis. And although the Consulting Service proved a transitory thing, there were lessons in it.

Establishment of the consulting service had come in 1956, and to its first-year operations the Fund for the Advancement of Education contributed $15,000. French, appointed director, submitted a projected budget of $26,000, and a questionnaire sent to the presidents of 484 institutions had suggested that more than a third would use such a service "at reasonable cost." Thus the effort was launched, its offices at Wellesley, where French had been chief business officer since 1954. The first year passed, then another. By 1958 a special committee of the federation board was overseeing operations while French was working valiantly to service institutional clients and to promote interest elsewhere. Because there was not a federation office, Wellesley was headquarters until 1959 for both the consulting service and the second sixty-college study. French resigned in 1959, to be succeeded briefly by George Van Dyke; but by 1960 the consulting service losses had reached $10,000, and the federation board felt that the effort should be liquidated. It was.[6]

As for the lessons, what were they? There had been a nervous feeling in the beginning, apparently, that a federation consulting program would compete, perhaps unfairly, with services offered by the commercial or public accounting firms. And of course there was the matter of professional "spread." Across what spectrum could a federation of business officers provide the definitive kinds of consultation a college might need? What, finally, was "reasonable cost" for the services that were offered? The questions were there, and they might need answering later.

Long before the second quinquennial assembly in 1960, there was arising talk of national association with, perhaps, a national office or, at least, a "national secretary" in Washington, D.C. In 1958, after a year of study, the executive committee of the Central Association recommended to the membership that the federation be replaced by a national association meeting every three years, the central responsibilities to be carried by a part-time staff member within the American Council. That year the Southern Association urged establishment of a national office for the existing federation. Other associations were equivocal or opposed, but the subjects were on the table. When the federation board held a special meeting in November 1958, it approved a motion authorizing "paid representation on a national basis" and appointment of a committee "to set up the format of a national headquarters." The daring of this proposal needs to be appreciated. In 1958 the federation dues were only $4 per year *per institution,* a suggested increase widely opposed. In 1960 the federation's income for the year was reported as $5,803.[7]

A stage had been set, and it was at this juncture that a combination of pressures—for creation of a national association, for establishment of representation in Washington, for closer ties to the American Council, and for improved contacts with federal agencies in the area of sponsored research—began to create events.

In 1959 the chairman of what was now called the federation's Standing Committee on Governmental Relations was George W. Green of Caltech, who was well acquainted with the costing and policy questions that still lay ahead of the research institutions (Circular A-21 was only a year old) and who had observed somewhat restlessly the slowness of the federation's movement toward truly effective national representation. Green believed that problems facing the committee would not wait and that, pending federation decisions on structure, the committee should have its own office in Washington with a director in constant contact with federal agencies. His solution was to invite, from institutions most directly in need of the committee's services, voluntary financial support of such an office. The committee would continue to have its professional base in the federation, but the financing would be its own. Late in 1959 Green presented the idea to his committee associates, and—because the committee's proposed role needed to be quite clear—discussed the implications with President Arthur S. Adams of the American Council and with Lee A. DuBridge, president of Caltech and then also president of the Association of American Universities. The plan was understood and approved. In January 1960 Green's proposal was approved by the federation board at a special meeting in the American Council headquarters at 1785 Massachusetts Avenue, N.W., Washington, D.C. Thirty-five institutions had pledged financial support—$2,500 per year for those with more than $2.5 million in federally sponsored research, $1,500 for others. The committee could proceed to choose a director, and Purdue's Robert Stewart headed the selection subcommittee.[8]

It would seem almost providential, in retrospect, that the man who became the committee's executive director was Nelson Wahlstrom, for Wahlstrom embodied depths of experience that were quite as important to the federation as to its standing committee. Wahlstrom had been thirty-two years at the University of Washington, more than half that time as its chief business officer, familiar with the financial exigencies of an institution that was, by 1960, among the top universities in federally funded research activities. Wahlstrom would be a new man in Washington, D.C., but few knew better than he the federal offices and policies with which he would be dealing or the issues before the institutions he would be representing. It was even more important that Wahlstrom knew the regional associations and the leaders of the federation. He had been a leader himself, president of the Western Association in 1951-52, director of the federation in 1951-53, secretary-treasurer in 1953-55, and president in 1955-57, when he had appointed that first committee to improve liaison with the American Council. Wahlstrom was in fact serving as a member of George Green's committee when he decided, at the urging of Green,

23

Stewart, and the others, to accept the new and experimental post
as the committee's full-time representative.* Resigning his university position, Wahlstrom went to Washington late in 1960, and by
January 1, 1961, had established a committee office in the Dupont
Circle Building near the American Council's Massachusetts Avenue
headquarters.[9]

What Green had achieved, and what Wahlstrom represented, was
immediate action toward establishment of an identifiable professional
address, action that otherwise might not have been accomplished for
years. Wahlstrom served a committee with a special mandate, but a
committee of the federation, its members the chief business officers of
their institutions and appointed by the president of the federation—
points upon which Green had insisted. Committee membership carried with it a certain distinction. The committee's working sessions,
usually bimonthly, were attended only by members and consultants or
by American Council representatives or federal agency guests. The
committee's "annual meetings," devoted to detailed reports of committee activities, were open only to the designated representatives of
the supporting institutions. Yet Wahlstrom and the current committee
chairperson always presented general reports at regional association
meetings, and representatives of any federation institution could feel
they had a port of call, at least, in Washington. Not altogether because
Wahlstrom's office was there, but certainly because it became a visible
model, the federation could begin to visualize the services a future
federation office might offer.

At the second quinquennial assembly in 1960, a resolution had
urged action toward association, specifically a general meeting to
examine the prospects and, if these were favorable, to "formulate a
constitution." The proposal took a different form, however, for a
general meeting had seemed too costly. Instead, federation president
Charles Wheeler met in Chicago in January 1961 with representatives
of each of the business officer associations—Wendell G. Morgan,
Howard University, for the American; Robert G. Hoefer, University

---

*Serving with Green in 1960 were George Baughman, New York University; Paul V.
Cusick, M.I.T.; H. O. Farber, Illinois; William B. Harrell, Chicago; G. C. Henricksen,
Duke; W. H. Lane, Jr., Columbia; Gilbert L. Lee, Jr., Michigan; Duncan I. McFadden,
Stanford; James M. Miller, California; A. W. Peterson, Wisconsin; Clarence Scheps,
Tulane; L. Gard Wiggins, Harvard; W. M. Young, Princeton, and Wahlstrom. When
Wahlstrom became executive director, he was succeeded on the committee by James J.
Ritterskamp, Jr., Illinois Institute of Technology. James Corley, California, soon suc-
ceeded Miller, and Kenneth D. Creighton, Stanford, replaced McFadden. Raymond J.
Woodrow, Princeton, was the representative from the Engineering College Research
Council.

of Cincinnati, for the Central; Edward Cratsley for the Eastern; Clarence Scheps for the Southern; and Harry E. Brakebill, San Francisco State College, for the Western. From that meeting came a draft of proposed bylaws, compiled by Kenneth Dick, federation secretary, approved by the federation board on February 20, and circulated by Dick to the regional associations. By the end of 1961, regional approvals had been received. National association would replace national federation in 1962. It would be an association without the NAEB, the separation after a dozen years viewed with some regret, but not really unhappily, even by the NAEB itself.[10]

On June 23, 1962, members of the federation board met at the Writers' Manor, Denver, the meeting called by Wilbur Pierpont, who had succeeded Wheeler as president. There was federation business, including a report by Paul V. Cusick of M.I.T., chairman of the Committee on Governmental Relations, who proposed the names of six appointees to fill committee vacancies. Such matters attended to, the board acted on the national association—changing the name, adopting the bylaws as revised by Kenneth Dick, and approving the necessary corporate certificate. The national association finally was a fact. There was, now, a "NACUBO."[11]

3

1963-1969: An Office in Washington

THE NEW NATIONAL ASSOCIATION had inherited in 1962 certain obligations, commitments, opportunities, and projects-in-prospect.

One commitment—and viewed, perhaps, as a test of faith—was to plan and conduct in Pittsburgh in 1963, three years after the second quinquennial assembly, a national association membership meeting that would be the first under the new structure and the first of a new triennial series. The proposal for such a meeting had been approved by the federation board in October 1961, and the program chairman, Swarthmore's Edward Cratsley, was at work on details.[1]

A commitment of a different kind was to *College and University Business Administration*. The federation board had decided as early as 1959 that Volumes I and II should be revised as soon as possible, the American Council again agreeing to undertake to mobilize financial support while the business officers assembled a revision committee. A committee of nineteen had been gathered rather quickly under the chairmanship of Clarence Scheps, who had served with the executive committee for Volume II and whose personal contributions to the literature had included his 1949 text, *Accounting for Colleges and Universities*. But financial support, of course, had not come immediately. In 1962, by which time the Scheps committee was long in place, work on revision awaited financing, although the regional associations were pledging a total of $2,200 to the effort. To the professional quality of the result, the members of the business officer committee would be contributing, again, their time and their experience—most of the work volunteer, all of it ahead.[2]

But a specific link to the American Council had been realized by 1962, a link more than symbolic. Since 1959 the federation board had explored possible ways to enlarge relationships with the council, represented until then only by the mutual interest in publication and revision of Volumes I and II. Soon an agreement was worked out whereby the council's business manager, Fred S. Vorsanger, would initiate an information service for business officers and would perform liaison functions, attending federation meetings and reflecting at council staff meetings the federation's interest in policy developments. Vorsanger published a quarterly *Newsletter* mailed to the some

26

700 business officers on federation lists, and his liaison role—which naturally included contact with Nelson Wahlstrom's committee programs—was well established by the time Logan Wilson succeeded Arthur Adams as president of the council in 1961. It was an important aspect of the new relationship that business officer boards and committees now could hold their meetings in the council's headquarters on Massachusetts Avenue.[3]

If members of the national association needed an occasion at which to celebrate their new status, the 1963 meeting in Pittsburgh provided it. The attendance was strong—more than 300 were registered for the July 14-17 session at the Pittsburgh Hilton—and so was the program, even though two of the principal speakers, one of them Logan Wilson (who sent the text of his address), were forced into last-minute cancellations. Panel sessions were built about a central theme of business office organization, and at the final dinner the speaker was Henry Heald, president of the Ford Foundation. There was a happy feeling that the national association was well launched.[4]

The launching had been done during the presidency of Wilbur Pierpont, and officers serving with him in 1962-63 had been Kenneth A. Dick, vice president; J. W. Bryant, now of Hampton Institute, secretary; and Trent C. Root of Southern Methodist University, treasurer. But one of the determinations at the assembly was to make future meetings biennial, the next national meeting in 1965, and the new national program would be until then under the direction of President Dick, who succeeded Pierpont. Bryant remained as secretary, but the new vice president was Scheps, and the treasurer R. D. Strathmeyer of the Carnegie Institute of Technology.*

Not the least of the developments of that spring and summer of 1963 was that Wahlstrom's committee offices had been moved into the American Council's building, for this move, too, was more than symbolic. For more than two years Wahlstrom had been working alone, with the help of a single secretary, in the Dupont Circle Building—keeping in touch with federal agencies as circumstances required and

---

*Members of the NACUBO board in 1963-64 were: *American Association:* Bryant, I. T. Creswell of Fisk, and A. L. Palmer of Texas Southern; *Central Association:* Pierpont, Carl A. Kasten of Drake, and James J. Ritterskamp, Jr. of Illinois Tech; *Eastern Association:* Cratsley, Strathmeyer, and Hertzfeld; *Southern Association:* Scheps, W. Ellis Jones of Florida, and Eugene H. Cohen, Miami; and *Western Association:* Dick, Conrad, and Brakebill. New members the following years would be B. A. Little, Southern University; Joseph A. Franklin, Indiana; Donald Murray, Pennsylvania; Luther C. Callahan, Alabama; and E. E. Davidson, Mississippi.

sending to the committee's supporting institutions the periodic reports of committee meetings and notes on legislative developments. But by April 1963, space had been found at 1785 Massachusetts Avenue, where Wahlstrom could be in close touch with President Wilson and members of the council staff—at first with Charles G. Dobbins, a senior member then directing the Commission on Federal Relations, later with John F. Morse, who came from a congressional office to assume that responsibility, and continuingly with Vorsanger, still the primary liaison officer. With the pressure for information steadily growing, Wahlstrom by that time had been given committee approval to recruit an information assistant, and this proved to be Neal O. Hines who, although not a business officer, had been director of information and university relations at the University of Washington and a long-time associate of Wahlstrom's. Committee reports were going that year from the new Massachusetts Avenue address to representatives of almost sixty research institutions now in the committee's enlarging circle.*

From the later 1950s, Kenneth Dick had been active in the affairs of his Western Association, then as an officer of the federation, and a participant in—and spokesman for—the creation of the national association. The question of the national office always had been moot, discussed many times in regional meetings, the results mixed, as in support by the Southern Association in 1959, opposition by the Central in the same year. But by 1964 the mood was changing, the advantages of a central headquarters more widely apparent. Vorsanger's *Newsletter* was national, if still of limited circulation because of the difficulty of maintaining proper mailing lists. Dues were collected by the regional associations to be remitted to the national treasurer, but the level of the annual payments (now $10 per institutional member) was beginning to seem absurdly low, even for an association without an office. An arrangement had been made with Wahlstrom for the housing of national association records, a clear hint that a central repository was important. And association board and committee members meeting in American Council facilities were tasting the interests implicit in that connection. There was no rush to the move-

---

*Wahlstrom's office on the first floor of the American Council building was one of about a dozen education association offices with which the council shared space. The gracious old building, later the headquarters of the National Trust for Historic Preservation, was itself of historic interest as the one-time Washington address of Secretary of the Treasury Andrew W. Mellon, who had assembled in his apartment there the first of the Old Master and other paintings eventually constituting the core of the priceless collection of the National Gallery of Art, which Mellon endowed.

ment, but by 1964 an association Committee on Plans and Objectives had recommended a study, and by 1965 President Dick was chairman of a special committee drafting a "guide" for further discussion.

It is useless to speculate on how events of sweeping national importance affected the attitudes of business officers in that two-year period between the association's first national meeting in 1963 and its second, which would be held at the Edgewater Beach Hotel in Chicago on July 11-13, 1965. But the history-making events of that era had profound effects on higher education, and business officers shared the rolling effects. The assassination of President Kennedy in November 1963 not only stunned the nation but threw into uncertainty and reorganization many of the new projects that had brought excitement and hope, especially to young people of college or new-career age. When President Johnson came to office, there would appear the beginnings of what proved a tragically mixed legacy—on the one hand new higher education legislation of landmark character, with mandates for educational development and vast new fundings for student loans and facilities, and on the other hand the seemingly irrevocable enlargement of the war in Vietnam, a war that would scar the national consciousness for years. And in this period, in 1964, came a burst of student violence at the University of California, the forerunner of other such incidents on many campuses and an episode that would make "Berkeley" a code word for student activism for the next decade. If not in that era, then soon, many institutions that had felt little touched by activities "in Washington" were feeling, surely, a need for the comfort of collective understanding.

The Dick committee's draft "guide" was an outline for discussion, but the paper submitted to the Committee on Plans and Objectives for its meeting in Chicago on April 19, 1965 set out in bold relief the need for a national office and the benefits that would accrue. The committee had expressed the hope that an office might be established by January 1, 1966, its executive a business officer of "first-class ability," its functions coordinated with those of the Committee on Governmental Relations, and its funding "in the range of $50,000 to $60,000 . . . to guarantee a quality operation." The Dick committee—with Wahlstrom an adviser and the members including Cusick, Scheps, Cratsley, Brakebill, and H. O. Farber of Illinois—went on from there. The group pointed out that the association needed to be "catching up" with other professional groups, including those related to the business field; that in no other way could business officers advance their professional objectives, establish necessary contacts with federal and state agencies, or sponsor the programs of institutional research or management improvement and training that were at the top of their pro-

29

fessional obligations. An annual budget of $70,000 was suggested, support coming in institutional dues payments of $50 to $150 based on the "size" (enrollment) of the member institution.* The Dick group thought that an executive vice president could be selected by June 1966 and the office opened shortly thereafter, possibly in the American Council's headquarters.[5]

Nothing happened that soon, of course. The national board apparently had no reservations about a Washington office (it had approved the recommendations of the Committee on Plans and Objectives in January 1965), but the regional association members seemingly were not altogether persuaded, the prospective rise in dues probably a factor. The Chicago meeting of 1965 came and went, and it was, like that at Pittsburgh, well organized and well attended, the program (William S. Kerr of Northwestern the chairman) putting emphasis on "Meet Your Federal Agencies" panels devoted to current problem areas such as college housing, student aid, facilities planning, and contract policies of the Navy, the Air Force, the Agency for International Development, and other offices. There was a joint meeting of the national board and regional association officers, but no discernible movement toward organization of a central staff. An important professional program was born, however. The board projected an annual workshop for senior business officers, a workshop that would become in time a keystone of the national workshop program.[6]

A national office was not yet realized, but in many ways the year 1965, far more than the year 1963, was one for approaches to decisions of long-term import.

Long before the association's Chicago meeting, it had been known that Wahlstrom would be retiring from his Committee on Governmental Relations post and returning to Seattle. A successor would have to be selected, and none knew where someone of that experience or potential might be found. Wahlstrom had been five years in a position that he had accepted on an experimental basis in 1960. By 1965 the experimental period was long over, the committee—always a "working committee," as in George Green's original design—firmly established in the Washington scene. The committee had matured. Since 1961 a representative of the Engineering College Research Council had been participating in its programs. In 1962 the member-

---

*In preparation for the meeting, Wahlstrom made a study by "size" of the 889 institutions then on regional and national association lists. About half, 438, had enrollments under 2,000. There were 303 with enrollments of 2,000 to 5,000, 113 with enrollments of 5,000 to 15,000, and just 35 with enrollments over 15,000.

ship had been expanded from fifteen to eighteen to permit appointment of research administrators competent to deal with the technical problems increasingly encountered. It was of particular importance that the committee's efforts were well synchronized with those of the American Council's Commission on Federal Relations and its Committee on Sponsored Research.* The committee's annual meetings were attended by as many as 175 institutional representatives, and the regular working sessions were attracting so many "observers" that controls eventually had to be imposed. Much of the success was due to Wahlstrom, a big man, mild in manner but a confident and tireless spokesman on issues of committee concern—never suggesting that he spoke for higher education at large (the American Council did that), but working within a well-defined sphere that was recognized as of great importance to higher education. In five years Wahlstrom had won for the committee not merely identity, but respect among the federal agencies and, widely, among major educational and research institutions, whether or not they were participating in the committee's financial support. Wahlstrom's successor would have much to live up to.[7]

With the 1965 situation thus—the Committee on Governmental Relations office exceedingly active, the national association office not yet in prospect—certain at-the-right-time developments put decisions on track.

Wahlstrom's successor was Howard P. Wile who, like Wahlstrom, came to the Washington office from the committee itself, thoroughly familiar with the committee's operations and policies. But Wile also was a research administrator possessing the special experience the committee had needed after 1962. An alumnus of Dartmouth and the Harvard Graduate School of Business Administration, Wile had been with M.I.T. laboratories during World War II and then had become administrator of research at Brooklyn Polytechnic, where he had served since 1946. Not the least of Wile's qualifications was that he was skillful in communication, quite able to develop in his own way the essential relationships with federal agencies, the committee institu-

---

*There had been serious talk in 1962 of making the Committee on Governmental Relations a specific agency of the American Council—perhaps in a "merger" of the committee with the Council's Commission on Sponsored Research, Wahlstrom becoming a council staff member. The decision on both sides by 1963 was that the mutual objectives would be better served if the committee maintained its independent status, functioning as a NACUBO program "working in harmony" with the council. Even before this matter had been resolved, George Green had died unexpectedly in 1962 at the age of 47, his loss mourned and his counsel much missed.

tions, and the American Council commissions. By September 1965, Wile was in his new position, and his secretary was Dorothy Kolinsky, new to the office but destined to make a career there. The committee chairman was Lytle Freehafer of Purdue.[8]

But it was of particular significance, so far as the association was concerned, that the new national president, Kenneth Dick's successor, was Clarence Scheps, whose election had been confirmed at Chicago. Scheps had just completed a two-year term as chairman of the Committee on Governmental Relations, actively involved in all developments following the committee's early contacts with the American Council and the move of the office to the American Council building. Scheps thus represented experience in the three most important ways—with the federation-cum-association, with the Committee on Governmental Relations, and with the council, where he was well known, in any case, as chairman of the committee on revision of Volumes I and II. The revision project was in motion, at last, the council having been assured of support from half a dozen foundations and other agencies.* It would have been impossible to find a president whose preparation was in better balance. If the association was to have a national office, the details would be worked out in Scheps's administration; his fellow officers were James J. Ritterskamp, Jr., now of Vassar, vice president; B. A. Little of Southern University, secretary; and W. A. Zimmerman of the University of Oregon Medical School, treasurer.**

The decisions regarding the national office and selection of an executive would come at the 1967 meeting of the association in New Orleans, which was, although the circumstance was only coincidental,

---

*National association representatives on the revision committee were Edward Cratsley, Swarthmore; Kenneth D. Creighton, Stanford; Kenneth R. Erfft, Duquesne; Lytle Freehafer, Purdue; W. C. Freeman, Texas A & M; Robert B. Gilmore, Caltech; Richard L. Helbig, Cazenovia; G. C. Henricksen, Duke; Paul W. Hodson, Utah; Gilbert L. Lee, Jr., Chicago; B. A. Little, Southern; Bruce J. Partridge, Johns Hopkins; James J. Ritterskamp, Jr., Vassar; and Daniel D. Robinson, Peat, Marwick, Mitchell & Co. The American Institute of Accountants (not yet AICPA) was represented by Ralph S. Johns of Haskins & Sells and Howard A. Withey of Peat, Marwick. Fred Vorsanger represented the American Council.

**Directors for 1965-67 were: *American Association:* Little, M. Maceo Nance, Jr. of South Carolina State College, and R. B. Welch of West Virginia State College; *Central Association:* Ritterskamp, J. A. Franklin of Indiana, and C. F. McElhinney of Houston; *Eastern Association:* Donald Murray of Pennsylvania, John F. Meck of Dartmouth, and Vincent Shea of Virginia; *Southern Association:* Scheps, E. E. Davidson of Mississippi, and Luther Callahan of Alabama; and *Western Association:* Zimmerman, Brakebill, and Kenneth D. Creighton.

the home ground of Tulane's Clarence Scheps. But one of the questions that invariably arose touched the matter of the future relationships between the Committee on Governmental Relations office, now well established, and a new office serving the larger association membership. This question, at least, had been faced squarely by 1966.

There was no doubt about physical arrangements. The association would share space with the committee in the American Council building. But a statement of philosophy was needed, and this statement had been drafted by a Committee on Governmental Relations subcommittee and approved by the committee on June 21, 1966. The statement, titled "Philosophical Concepts," said that there should be "a single coordinated office" with "staff and all activities . . . under the supervision of the executive vice president." There should be "no diminution of the activities within the areas now encompassed by the Committee on Governmental Relations," its supporting institutions continuing "to bear an appropriate portion of the costs" of the office. The goal was to create a national headquarters "so structured as to permit it to represent ultimately all aspects of the business and financial administration of colleges and universities."[9]

There had been many preliminary consultations and, of course, talks within the association about who might be considered a prospect for executive vice president. Preparations for the New Orleans meeting, to be held July 16-18, 1967 at the Jung Hotel, had proceeded for months, always in the knowledge that the national office issue would be faced again. But a month before the meeting it was known that plans for the office needed only to be confirmed and that, as Fred Vorsanger announced in what would be the final issue of his *Newsletter*, the new executive vice president would be Kenneth Dick, the choice of a search committee headed by Ritterskamp. The program of the meeting itself was, again, a strong one, the program committee under the chairmanship of Luther Callahan, Alabama, having balanced the general sessions (one of them, significantly, dealing with "Tensions on the Campus") with a new round of "Meet Your Federal Agencies" panels arranged with the help of Howard Wile. (Wile also enlisted two of the principal speakers, Juan Trippe of Pan American Airways and Rep. Emilio Q. Daddario of Connecticut.) At the business meeting, the office and the Dick appointment were confirmed. When the officers and directors for 1967-69 held their meeting on July 19, it was time to start planning for operations at levels never attained before. A participant in the planning would be Ernest Conrad, new chairman of the Committee on Governmental Relations.[10]

The national office was opened in September 1967 by the newcomer to Washington. The office shared the far-from-commodious space of Howard Wile's committee quarters in the American Council building. It also shared Neal Hines, still working with the Committee on Governmental Relations information program, now to devote up to half his time to association affairs. Budget allocations (for the nine months after September) totaled $74,000, including $35,570 for salaries and benefits, $19,000 for administrative travel, and $2,500 for a new national publication of some kind. Annual dues, based on enrollments and collected by the regional associations for transmission to the national office, would range from $60 for institutions with fewer than 1,000 students to $200 for those with more than 15,000. As for overall administration, the new office was to begin to operate under the terms outlined in the Committee on Governmental Relations' memorandum of June 21, 1966, which the national board specifically approved by reference at its July 19 meeting.[11]

To Kenneth Dick the move to Washington was a culmination of almost two decades of work for the federation and association. Dick was a westerner with B.S. and M.S. degrees from the University of Idaho, an M.B.A. from Stanford, and a professional career that had begun at Idaho in 1931 and made him in time Idaho's vice president for financial affairs. Of the appropriateness of his selection there was no doubt, for Dick had been for at least a decade a leading spokesman first for the association and then for the establishment of the central office which he now would direct.

Behind Dick was a board that wanted to see things go. The new national president, after Scheps, was Ritterskamp, the new vice president Kenneth D. Creighton of Stanford, Little remaining as secretary and Zimmerman as treasurer. New to the board were Robert B. Gilmore of Caltech from the Western Association; Keith L. Nitcher of Kansas from the Central; Harold K. Logan, now of Tuskegee, from the Southern; and Thomas A. McGoey of Columbia from the Eastern. Interest and support were there. The future, as the saying went, lay ahead.

Dick's term as executive vice president was of two years—from his arrival at the new office after the 1967 New Orleans meeting until his departure after a highly successful national meeting in San Francisco's Sheraton-Palace Hotel in 1969. It was a biennium of beginnings, of "firsts," of adjustments in budget, operations, and staff, and—at one tragically memorable moment—of efforts to function in a Washington that was, literally, burning.

The office was assuming in 1967 many of the financial and record-keeping chores that had been passed around for years; but beyond the housekeeping, the first task was to begin to communicate with a national membership that was far from perfectly identified. The communication was begun, nevertheless, by publication in October of a new bimonthly newsletter called, somewhat obviously, *College and University Business Officer*. Five of these were issued in 1967-68 with the $2,500 funding set up in the initial budget, but before that first year was out, *Business Officer* was going to some 2,500 representatives of about 1,000 institutions identified (by the regional associations) as members. Mailing lists were constantly changing, but *Business Officer* was well recognized. In September 1968, a new publication schedule called for ten issues per year.[12]

It was indicative of the range of pressures facing the office that new projects were crowding old ones, that important new committees were approved but not immediately appointed, that not all programs got off in step. Yet new committees were created (some absorbing overloads in the Committee on Governmental Relations), and a single-volume revision of *College and University Business Administration* was nearing publication. The structure of the association was about to change, too. In 1968 the American Association would dissolve itself after almost thirty years, when black business officers could bring their institutions into the ranks of the regionals. It was fitting that one of the association's first sponsored projects was designed to encourage and promote sound business practices in the black colleges, and that from such activities came publications and workshops that proved to be models for later professional efforts.*

As early as January 1968, the national board approved the creation of three new committees, one for small colleges, others on publications and professional development. The Small Colleges Committee soon was off and running under the chairmanship of William T. Haywood of Mercer University, developing in frequent meetings plans and proposals of interest to the four-year liberal arts institutions which, although heavily represented in the membership, never had been given such attention before. But the Publications and Professional Development committees were not appointed for a year—W. A. Zimmerman would head Publications and Scheps, Professional Development—and in the meantime, President Ritterskamp, after consultations with the board, had appointed a Committee on Plans and Objectives, the chairman Vice President Creighton and his associates C. F. McElhinney of

---

*It should be noted that short courses and institutes for business officers had been conducted for many years. A summer short course at the University of Nebraska, Omaha, was in its nineteenth year in 1968, a University of Kentucky institute in its sixteenth, and the University of California, Santa Barbara, was holding its fifteenth. All had professional and regional association support.

Houston and Vincent Shea of Virginia. By early spring the committee was at work.[13]

What happened at that juncture—another national tragedy, the assassination of Martin Luther King, Jr.—was of dimensions too large to be thought of in connection with the separate shocks registered in a small Washington office or among the people it represented. Yet to college business officers, who were welcoming their American Association colleagues to memberships in the regional associations, the event in Memphis and the sequel in Washington would forever have a special meaning.

It had been known for a year that the American Association would be dissolved in 1968, the passage of years and the civil rights legislation of the 1960s having ended the separateness that had existed when black business officers organized in 1939. The American Association's national directors—B. A. Little, M. Maceo Nance, Jr. of South Carolina State College, and R. B. Welch of West Virginia State—would be the last to sit as representatives of the American, and a national board meeting scheduled in Washington on April 5-6, 1968—the day after a Committee on Governmental Relations working session—would be their next-to-last regular meeting. Little was president of the American as well as secretary of the national association.

The King assassination occurred in Memphis on April 4. By the following day, fires were burning in Washington, downtown areas were emptying, public transportation was almost nonexistent, and much inbound airline traffic was being rerouted or put on a turnaround basis.* But by midmorning, April 6, because a few directors already were in town—Little, Nance, and Welch among them—the national board did nevertheless try to hold its meeting on an upper floor of an almost-empty Statler Hilton Hotel in an almost-empty city. By noon the meeting was over. A quorum had been present—barely, since some directors had been halted at the airports—but it had not been a time to think about the plans and objectives report.

The American Association had been organized in an era in which its members, going to meetings, could not find lodging at most hotels. It was dissolved in the year a civil rights leader was shot down. That was coincidence. But when the dissolution came, the American created a living gift of professional significance. Late in the summer of 1968, President Little, as authorized by resolution, sent to the national association a check for $3,135.05, the balance of the American Associa-

---

*On April 4, government offices closed at 3:00 p.m., and a traffic jam ensued. Several COGR representatives, their meeting adjourned, directed traffic at 18th Street and Massachusetts Avenue from about 3:00 to 4:30 p.m.[14]

tion's funds, to be used to help improve business management at the black institutions.[15]

A year before the San Francisco meeting—that is, by mid-1968— plans for it were in motion. The Western Association would be host, and the national board was receiving regular reports from Western President Bo-Wilhelm Skarstedt of the University of the Pacific and from Harry Brakebill, now of the California State Colleges, program chairman. But on the professional front, projects of even longer range were in the works. One of them was a set of pilot workshops, conducted under the sponsorship of the U.S. Office of Education, for colleges participating in federal student financial aid programs. The other was a management improvement program designed specifically to serve the "predominantly Negro" institutions and funded by two $50,000 grants from the Esso Foundation.[16]

Of the two, the Esso-NACUBO program would be the most far-reaching in its effect. The original design had been discussed in 1966, polished in 1967, and now—with the national office in place—inaugurated. The object was to set up guidelines to improve planning and management. Under the first grant, five black colleges—Albany State, Florida Memorial, Jarvis Christian, Miles, and Wiley—were to receive consulting services by Peat, Marwick, Mitchell & Co. Under the second, the same services would be extended to five additional institutions: Grambling, Huston-Tillotson, Morehouse, Talladega, and Texas College. Eventually, manuals would be published—manuals useful to scores of other institutions of many sizes and types. Little headed the national association steering committee, other members including President Ritterskamp; Donald S. Murray, Pennsylvania; James W. Bryant, now with the Ford Foundation; and Kenneth R. Erfft, Duquesne.[17]

The one-volume revision of *College and University Business Administration,* the product of three years of accelerating work by the Scheps committee and an array of special consultants, was published by the American Council that June. The editors had been George Van Dyke and then John M. Evans of the University of Connecticut, who had headed the editorial subcommittee. Action had been proceeding since the council finally had been assured of funding for the project first visualized in 1959, the contributors including the council itself, the regional associations, the U.S. Office of Education, the Teachers Insurance and Annuity Association, and the U.S. Steel, IBM, Shell, and General Electric Foundations. The edition of 16,000, awaited so long, soon was sold out—but it was a measure of the new realizations that the association already was creating a new Manual Revision Committee, Robert Gilmore the chairman, which soon was developing plans for the next effort.[18]

The "Statement of Aims and Objectives" developed by Vice President Creighton's committee was approved by the board and distributed to member institutions in late summer of 1968 as a fourteen-page report setting out major goals and proposing a timetable for their achievement. The statement was detailed—the first comprehensive view of how the association might approach the opportunities spread before it—but it had come not too soon. Events were tending to overtake it. The timetable suggested programs phased through two five-year periods, but already it was probable that certain objectives not expected to be reached before 1973 might be attained by 1969-70.[19]

The administrative and housekeeping questions persisted, of course. A membership referendum late in 1968 approved association bylaws amendments redefining voting members, opening membership to nonprofit organizations (which would become associate members, paying half the maximum dues), and stipulating that a simple majority would constitute a quorum of the national board. But space in the national office had become a problem—the Committee on Governmental Relations and association activities still jostled into space once occupied only by the committee—and to provide temporary relief, the association took a short-term lease on an office in a nearby Georgetown University building where Hines worked with publications and mailing lists. It was known by 1968 that the American Council would be constructing or acquiring its own new headquarters, and the association/committee requirements were calculated in a preliminary way at about 2,500 square feet—a striking underestimate, as events would prove. And while the central staffing had been static (and secretarial assistance usually transient), Dick had brought to the office in 1969 a new permanent staff member, Sheila R. Sanjabi, a graduate of Georgetown and recently with COMSAT's International Division. Sanjabi, initially a secretary, soon was a special assistant to Dick, and recorder and records custodian for the national board.[20]

By early autumn of 1968, Dick had notified the national board of his intention to retire on September 1, 1969. By November, Vice President Creighton was chairman of another committee, a committee to search for Dick's successor, its members including Conrad, Cratsley, Little, McElhinney, and Scheps. By June 1969, a month before the San Francisco meeting, the choice had been made, approved by the board, and announced. The new executive vice president would be D. Francis Finn, since 1961 business manager and assistant treasurer at Purdue and, in fact, the new—and newly installed, in April—president of the Central Association.[21]

There would be time for the association-at-large to get acquainted with Finn, for he would go to the San Francisco meeting as executive vice president-elect. But Finn was, actually, already widely known, not only for his regional association services, but for early work with the NAEB and current work as a member of the Professional Development Committee headed by Scheps. His credentials were impressive— a B.A. from Brown (*cum laude* and Phi Beta Kappa) in economics, World War II army service abroad, graduate studies in international politics and statistics, and purchasing experience at Brown until his move to Purdue. It was significant that Finn's career had covered both business management and purchasing (he had drafted the chapter on purchasing for the 1968 revision of *College and University Business Administration*), and that he seemed invariably a leader in whatever programs or organizations called him. He was, finally, young enough to give the association's projects the energetic attention they would need.

The San Francisco meeting on July 13-15 was a showcase for programs gaining momentum. The meeting really was two, for a curtain-raiser was the Committee on Governmental Relations annual meeting, attended by more than 150 representatives, at which the principal speaker was Elmer Staats, comptroller general of the United States; reports were given by Howard Wile and the subcommittee chairpersons; and Ernest Conrad, finishing a two-year term, yielded the committee chairmanship to Robert F. Kerley, who was moving that month from the University of Kentucky to Johns Hopkins. When the association's meeting convened, more than 900 representatives, spouses, and guests were registered. Among speakers at that program were John Oswald, executive vice president, University of California; Elmer Jagow, long a well-known business officer and now president of Hiram College; and Glenn Dumke, chancellor of the California State Colleges—and all meetings and panel discussions were keyed to the theme of higher education in the 1970s. The participants expressed their thanks to Kenneth Dick and welcomed Francis Finn. The new national president was Kenneth Creighton, the vice president, Thomas McGoey, and the treasurer, Keith Nitcher. Harold Logan, who had succeeded Little as secretary in 1968, continued in that office. New directors were Robert W. Meyer, Ohio Wesleyan; Harold M. Myers, Drexel; and William Haywood, Mercer.[22]

Much work was ahead. Thirteen national committees (including the Committee on Governmental Relations, of course) were in action, several with particularly urgent questions before them. A dues increase almost certainly would be necessary soon, and President Creighton and his colleagues would have to present that proposition to the membership.

Meantime, it was of sentimental as well as professional importance that the resources of the national office were about to be expanded in special ways. J. Harvey Cain had given to the association his extensive files of books, papers, and records accumulated during almost forty years of work in the management field. The collection would become the core of a national library, and the library would be housed in the association's offices in the new American Council headquarters, which would be called the National Center for Higher Education.[23]

4

1970-1971: Defining the Professional

THE ASSOCIATION and its Committee on Governmental Relations entered the 1970s with offices in one of the new suites in the American Council building at One Dupont Circle. The move had been made on December 16, 1969, after anticipatory planning that had begun in Kenneth A. Dick's time, long before the San Francisco meeting. The layout was functional, offices for the small staff laid out about a central conference room that would contain the library, to which George Van Dyke now also had donated his collection. The projected national program was functional, too, but its ambitions already tended to expand those elements outlined so recently in the "Statement of Aims and Objectives." The thirteen committees now were fifteen, including certain "project committees" working on association affairs. More than ninety business officers constituted the committee forces in the field.

The 1966 plans committee had said that business officers should be "catching up." Since then, with the national office in place, the association had been doing so, as the San Francisco meeting demonstrated. Yet the challenge facing President Kenneth Creighton and his colleagues in 1970, with Francis Finn in the national office, was to set program priorities that would not merely help the association "catch up," but that would help equip business officers themselves to participate more effectively, singly or together, in the decision-making processes of higher education. The goals were, at their largest, to cultivate a wider sense of professionalism, then to expand the opportunities for professional service. But what or who was a professional? What were the incentives, obligations, rewards?

The literature was full of references to "professional ideals and standards," yet certain ambiguities always hung in the air. A profession, by common definition, was a vocation requiring specialized training, perhaps of a learned nature; admission, usually by examination; ethical standards of performance; and dedication to service beyond considerations of personal gain. Questions: How well did the college or university business officer fit the definition? What was "admission" to the profession? Appointment to a major position? Acknowledged experience? The winning of a higher academic degree? Above all, and

41

whatever the case, why was it that business officers, well trained, experienced, characteristically dedicated to service of impeccable ethical quality—professionals in most eyes—seemed so rarely to be winning places of professional parity in the highest councils of higher education? There were many M.B.A.s, but few Ph.D.s. There were increasing numbers of vice presidents for business and finance, but few college or university presidents from the business ranks. Who really was listening—*College and University Business Administration* notwithstanding—when business officers talked about "improving principles and practices of business and financial administration in higher education"? On what base did their authority rest?

Lloyd Morey, that archetype of the business office professional, had raised such questions in 1961. Morey, who held a doctorate and who was by that time president of the University of Illinois, touched the general problem in his reminiscent talk to old friends at his Central Association's golden anniversary meeting—and business officers, he thought, were not reaching high enough.

> "Some disappointment can be felt at the failure of educational organizations to include business officers in their major committees and policy-making groups. A very few have business officers committees in their lists. Rarely, however, is a business officer found in an executive or major policy committee. . . .
> "Perhaps it has been a feeling on the part of educational leaders that business administration is not a part of the educational operations and that finance is not a significant factor in educational decisions. Of the fallacy of both these premises there can be no doubt, and progress is being made in bringing about their correction. . . . (But) one of the less fortunate features of a career as business officer is that it is substantially a "closed-end" profession. In this respect the situation is different from that of most business concerns. . . .
> "More complete academic education, including a doctorate, broadening of outlook, participation in teaching as a member of the faculty, activity in research and writing, all increase the chances of a business officer to be well considered for a presidency. They also lift his stature among his academic colleagues, which is likewise to his advantage."[1]

It was not a presidency that the business officer usually sought, although by 1970 more were being selected. Elmer Jagow, at Hiram, was one. M. Maceo Nance, Jr. was president of his South Carolina State College. At the University of California (where a precedent had been set forty years before), Charles J. Hitch recently had been brought from the business office to succeed Chancellor Clark Kerr.* What the business officer had a right to expect, however—and what

---

* In the two-year period 1980-81 alone, at least twelve business officers became presidents of NACUBO member institutions.

the national association might provide—was the chance to think as a professional and to believe that his or her services deserved equal weight in the councils of higher education. It was significant that the "Statement of Aims and Objectives," in its section on professional development, spoke of "The Ideal of Professional Growth." The proposed activities:

1. Attracting many more able business and financial people to the field of higher education.
2. Further upgrading the education and proficiency of many already in the field.
3. Exploring the feasibility of *establishing standards of performance* for business and financial officers. (emphasis supplied)

Perhaps, definitions aside, professionalism was a point of view, a willingness to broaden the outlook, as Morey said. The doctorate—or the college presidency—was up to the individual. The opportunity for continuing learning was something the national association could do something about. It could whet the professional appetite.

But professional development, as the association could approach it, would require programs and projects of breadths rarely dreamed of before—general and particular institutional studies, workshops and critiques on wider scales, new circles of communication, publications of professional caliber. All required planning. Each would be expensive, the cost-effectiveness calculations for the future. Meantime, a proposed dues increase might help make it all possible.

The terms of the increase, and the need for it, had been thoroughly covered in *Business Officer* late in 1969, and the returns from a national mail balloting were due in Washington on December 16, the day the office was moved to One Dupont Circle. The increase was approved handily, 70 percent of the 966 member institutions responding, more than a majority in favor. On June 1, 1970, dues would rise from $60 to $100 for the smallest institutions and from $200 to $500 for those with enrollments over 15,000. At its January meeting the board immediately began to make plans for workshops, publications, and new membership services.[2]

The dues increase was important in itself, but the achieving of it was a revelation of how far the national association had come in scarcely more than half a dozen years. The member institutions, which once had weighed apprehensively the costs of a national office, now had a feeling for what advantages were accruing. And the change in mood had come at no sacrifice to the regional associations. The regionals

43

were, in fact, stronger. Their own meetings and workshops flourished.* Their representatives to the national board could help make plans for national efforts where these were needed while the regionals maintained their historic independence. A recommendation on a national issue, as in the decision to ask a dues increase, came from the national board. The balloting was national, each member institution casting its ballot through its "primary representative," usually the chief business officer. The system was clean and clear. The national association represented a regional association multiplied by four. But on national matters the member institutions spoke to the national. That had happened on the proposed dues increase for 1970.

A catalogue of projects-in-view in 1970 is a long one. Any reading of the record suggests the momentum that had been achieved. The "Statement of Aims and Objectives" still was the basic guide, but the pace of activity was due in large part to the presence of Francis Finn, whose orientation period had lasted no longer than the move to the new offices and who was busy on all fronts requiring staff attention. New committees included those on Cost Studies (which was developing a subcommittee—a "Grad-Cost" group—on the costs of graduate education), on Facility Construction, and on Student Aid (these taken over from the Committee on Governmental Relations); and on Investments, Insurance, Personnel, and Taxation. The Professional Development and Publications Committees were wrestling, sometimes jointly, with the large questions of professional communication. There was also a Membership Committee. The Esso-NACUBO group was maintaining contact with scheduled study sessions at the black colleges. Soon the association and Committee on Governmental Relations had established a joint committee on liaison with the Western Interstate Commission on Higher Education (WICHE), which was trying to develop a new management information system. Amid all this, workshops were blossoming, and the first serious effort at professional publications was launched.[3]

The first workshops touched each end of a wide spectrum. For many months William Haywood's Small Colleges Committee had been devising plans to meet the needs of the association's largest constituency. By February 1970, the committee was proceeding with arrangements for a series of workshops—at Atlanta, Columbus, Los Angeles, and Philadelphia—on planning, budgeting, and accounting for small

---

*It is noteworthy and revealing that, in a national association so new, constituent elements were celebrating 50th anniversaries. The Central Association's program of 1961 now had been followed by the Eastern's golden anniversary meeting of 1969.

44

colleges. The sessions, held in March and April, were instantly successful, but they also suggested a refinement. In new series planned for
1971, there were separate workshops on planning and budgeting and
on fund accounting. The texts in each case included the *Planning,
Budgeting, and Accounting* volume of the *College Operating Manual,*
made possible by a grant from the Ford Foundation and prepared by
Peat, Marwick, Mitchell & Co. under the sponsorship of Howard
University and Southern University. And in 1970 there was a senior
accounting workshop. The first in that annual series was held in
St. Louis in May under the auspices of the Professional Development
Committee.[4]

With so much going on, it had been apparent for months that a staff
addition would be necessary. The workshops required central coordination. Keeping the lines open to fifteen committees, some holding
frequent meetings, was an interesting and challenging aspect of staff
service. (Finn was attending many committee meetings and workshops
as well as the regional association annual meetings.) The office had
established a circulating library (guides and manuals for short-term
loan) and a consultant registry, a central listing of business officers
willing to engage in consulting services. Space in the national office
now was being shared with the American Association of Collegiate
Schools of Business, and other such arrangements, some closer to
association interests, were in view. By March 1970 a new staff member
had been selected; he was Jerry R. Anderson, of Augustana College,
whose assignment was to start coordinating the workshops and go
from there. But it was typical of the times that another change came
almost at once. By July 1970 Anderson had been named executive
director of the College and University Personnel Association, which
had leased space in the business officers' headquarters. Anderson's
successor was Sheila Sanjabi, already in the office, since 1969 the
secretary-assistant to Kenneth Dick and Francis Finn, and now confirmed by the national board as staff associate, a professional entry
position. Sanjabi, a graduate in languages, had prepared herself, even
as a secretary, by taking evening work in accounting. She now would
handle the workshops and much else, not least the central coordination, year by year, for the association's annual meetings.[5]

By mid-1970 additional committees had been appointed. One was
a Long-Range Planning Committee headed by Vice President Mc-
Goey, who also was chairman of the Committee on Plans and Objectives. A Committee on Ethics was headed by Edward Cratsley, a
Bylaws Committee by Merl M. Huntsinger, Washington University.
The national board already was looking forward to the 1971 national
meeting, which would be held in New York—the last of the biennial

45

meetings, the first of the annual—and committees on program and site were at work under Chairmen Paul R. Linfield, Franklin and Marshall, and Robert W. Meyer, Ohio Wesleyan.[6]

But what was being done about professional publication? Developments were coming, and they were interesting because they were the association's unique responses to its needs at that stage. In professional publication the needs were for flexibility and time for proper cultivation. The solutions provided both.

From the earliest days of the national office, the association had anticipated that, when the time was ripe, there would be a quarterly professional journal. W. A. Zimmerman's Publications Committee had discussed this. A journal was one of the objectives in the "Statement" of 1969. But nothing had happened because a regular publication of professional caliber was, of course, a perpetual commitment for which the association was not ready. At the national office a journal would mean allocation of incalculable costs in production and staff time. In the field, there was no habit of professional inquiry even though the magazine *College and University Business* still provided an outlet for the papers and reports that were being done. (There was, in fact, some feeling that business officers would not "write," although the pertinent question was whether business officers had contributions to make.) It was Clarence Scheps's Professional Development Committee that suggested an answer in 1969. Why not, the committee asked, institute a series of occasional papers presenting, singly, the best of the studies coming along—papers issued on no fixed schedule but in uniform format and capable of being preserved in the business officer's own files? The result, early in 1970, was the inception of the NACUBO *Professional File*—the name selected to indicate, it was hoped, both the professional level of the materials and the expectation of their preservation. By March the first paper had been published, and by July, the fourth. The separate issues were keyed for filing ("Accounting," "Administration," "Investment," and so on). The idea was catching on. The commitment in cost was minimal. The series was monitored by the Publications Committee, Vincent Shea, Virginia, the chairman after January 1970.[7]

Flexibility had solved the "journal" problem. It would help solve another, although in this case much time and cultivation of activity across the widest range of administrative interests would be necessary.

At the core of the matter of professional activity, publications included, was a circumstance only rarely recognized in higher education and seemingly accepted by business officers as a fact of life, no thanks expected. Business officers were forever in support of something—

46

their institutions, the American Council, national commissions of one kind or another. Their contributions—as with *College and University Business Administration*—were contributions of the purest kind, work done for the general good and without regard to preferment or "personal gain," to recall the definition of the professional. The individual business officer's personal advancement came with experience and demonstrated capacity. What one did beyond was from interest, pride, or a need for self-satisfaction. As for publication, business officers, unlike their academic colleagues, faced no "publish or perish" pressures. But the opposite side of that coin was that they were not even accustomed to having an outlet for work judged rigorously by their peers. The association now was trying to provide the outlet, and soon it would be asking larger numbers of business officers to support, again, that largest project of all—the further revision of "the manual." The effort would go in new directions.

Caltech's Robert Gilmore was chairman of the Manual Revision Committee that already was laying plans for the further revision of the 1968 single-volume revision of *College and University Business Administration*. Gilmore's colleagues were William C. Erskine, Colorado; Gilbert L. Lee, Jr., now of Chicago; E. E. Davidson, now of Oklahoma State; and Kurt M. Hertzfeld, Amherst. But a need for a committee dealing exclusively with accounting already had been perceived, and so in autumn 1970, President Creighton had appointed an Accounting Principles Committee, its chairman Gilbert Lee, and Gilmore a member *ex officio*. Serving with Lee were Carl W. Janke, Harvard; Wilbur Pierpont, Michigan; Norman H. Gross, California; W. Harold Read, Tennessee; and Caspa L. Harris, Jr., Howard. All planning was of specific interest, obviously, to Scheps's Professional Development Committee and to Vincent Shea's Publications Committee, but virtually all of the program committees also would be involved—Cost Studies, under Loren M. Furtado, California; Personnel, Orie E. Myers, Jr., Emory; Investments, John F. Meck, Dartmouth; Insurance, David R. Baldwin, Wayne State; and others.[8]

What came from the Manual Revision Committee late in 1970 was an entirely new plan, a plan that would make revision an evolutionary process involving publications at four levels. The *Professional File*, using top-of-the-line papers, would be a "testing ground" for ideas and explorations of principle. The specialized manuals, such as *Planning, Budgeting, and Accounting*, would provide testing in another way, through exposure to discussions at workshops. (The *PBA* manual was about to be followed by a *Student Records Manual* flowing from the Peat, Marwick work with the Esso-NACUBO program.) But there would come, then, a *College and University Business Administration* in two

47

forms. The first would be a chapter-by-chapter revision, the chapters issued separately for incorporation into a looseleaf publication called the Administrative Service, this to keep information perpetually current. Finally, there would be later single-volume issues incorporating the chapters as most recently revised, the first of these probably in 1975. The Administrative Service would be distributed by subscription, the later books as true "manuals."[9]

In professional publication, flexibility had become the rule. The *Professional File* would be published when something worth publishing had been accepted. The Administrative Service would be that way too. It was remarkable how soon business officers (who some had feared would not "write") were participating so widely in writings and discussions that were of the essence of professional activity.

So 1971 came, and with it new kinds of challenges to management in new kinds of problems and, in November, the national association's annual meeting in New York—a fine meeting in which the talks and panel discussions could only struggle to keep abreast of changes affecting higher education.

Colleges and universities that were surprised by the 1960s were still groping for help in the 1970s. Some of the developments were legal and technical, as when the Department of Labor, after passage by Congress of the Employment Security Amendments of 1970, was working on unemployment insurance guidelines that would affect the colleges. But there were larger issues, some far from resolution. There was anxiety about what was called "campus unrest" (a President's Commission had made a study of the problem in 1970), and incidents of violence were occurring, most in protest of the Nixon administration's seeming slowness in winding down the Vietnam War. (The "unrest" erupted in Washington in May 1971, when thousands of protestors flooded the city, and one of the mobilization areas was Dupont Circle, at the front door of the National Center for Higher Education.) The "campus unrest" was bad enough, but one of the peripheral effects on most campuses was an increase in insurance rates to cover incidental damage. All institutions were facing financial uncertainties, but the black colleges particularly were in severe straits—described by their leaders as the "invisible American institutions," chronically shortchanged in the allocations of funds for teaching and research. Institutions had been maintaining after 1965 new programs designed, in response to the Civil Rights Act of 1964 and Executive Order 11246 in 1965, to end racial and other discrimination in employment. By August 1971, just before the beginning of the new academic year, the Nixon administration's wage-price freeze was imposed by executive order, and a new Cost of Living Council was making policy decisions and issuing interpretations and guidelines. Like the American Council, the offices of the association were dealing in that season, by telephone and by letter, with hundreds of requests for information. The eight-page *Business Officer* was increasingly filled with reports and short articles on Washington developments and analyses of special issues under study by association committees. Soon the association established a bulletin service in a new medium called NACUBO *Special Report.*[10]

What also was happening, and what had been happening, almost without anyone's realizing its meaning, was that the business officers, so close to the front lines in the new period of pressures on management, were becoming the focus for higher education's forces in the field. The sheer spread of the association's committee structure reflected the expanded range of higher education's management concerns, and any higher education association or office, or any federal agency, could find among the association's committees the elements of interest and experience not readily available elsewhere. Yet there was a concurrent development of equal significance. Business officers prominent in the association's work were being invited in larger numbers to serve as members of the boards, commissions, and committees of other established national organizations—the American Council, first of all, but also the Association of American Universities, the National Association of State Universities and Land-Grant Colleges, many others—and of movements of the kind represented by WICHE. Such business officers, working outside the association framework, nevertheless were performing at the national level their classic campus role—offering their special expertise in approaches to new problems. The cumulative effect, if difficult to measure, unquestionably was important when so many organizations were having to orient their thinking in management fields. Higher education's searches for policy or position—particularly when responses to federal offices were required—could only have been sharpened by such experienced support.

The association's directors, committee members, and much of the membership looked toward the national meeting with special interest that year. The meeting would be held on November 21-23, 1971, at New York's Waldorf-Astoria, which was interesting enough (the dates had been established with regard to the traditional meeting time of the Eastern Association, the host), but there were other reasons. The year had made business officers hungry for straight talk about issues before them. The theme of the meeting—the program being put together by Paul Linfield's committee—was "The Management Challenge: Now and Tomorrow." The theme fit the time. But other plans were ripening, too.

The New York meeting was to be held in late autumn, yet national officers were to be elected by the board at its annual summer session. Thus it was on June 22, 1971, that Thomas McGoey was elected president to succeed Kenneth Creighton—and thus it was, further, that McGoey, who had announced in April his retirement from Columbia in July, would serve only a month as president, then remain on the board for a year as an *ex officio* member. To succeed McGoey, the board elected Harold M. Myers, of Drexel University, who would head the association until the second annual meeting to be held in Denver in July 1972. The new vice president was William T. Haywood, Mercer, still deep in work with the Small Colleges Committee; the secretary, Merl M. Huntsinger, Washington University; and the treasurer, Glen E. Guttormsen, San Jose State College.[11]

The board meeting that June was in its way a national meeting in miniature, an occasion for program review and for launching what proved to be an historic and continuing interaction with other associations in fields related to university business affairs.

The program developments had been striking. The membership had approved, in another mail ballot, amendments to the bylaws permitting new or not-yet-accredited institutions to enter the association as provisional members, paying regular dues but without vote until they joined the regular ranks. The association thus could offer publications and other services to developing institutions at the times they might be most valuable. There was, in addition, a new Community Colleges Committee—the chairman William B. Cutler, of California's Foothill Junior College District—which would be, for the moment, a subcommittee of the Membership Committee, enlisting interest among the two-year institutions. Gilbert Lee's Accounting Principles Committee, tooling up its long-range program, had established liaison with the American Institute of Certified Public Accountants and its Committee on Audits of Educational Institutions. (The time was near when the association would be deeply involved in review of the AICPA's projected audit guide.) The Insurance Committee, under the leadership of David Baldwin, was far advanced in a program that had begun with a survey of institutions in 1970, had been enlarged by the development of basic guidelines, and had included two meetings in Washington with selected representatives of the insurance industry. The committee already was projecting preparation of a risk management manual for higher education.[12]

But that June board meeting was itself noteworthy as the starting

50

point of what would become the Interassociation Management-Related Group, from which would flow a number of new cooperative ventures, among them a Higher Education Administration Referral Service (HEARS). The directors were joined that time by the presidents of the regional associations, the chairmen of the national committees, and the representatives of twelve "business-related" organizations, many of them old friends (Bert Ahrens, of NAEB, for example), but many the officers of newer groups, such as the insurance managers, the college and university planners, and others. The meeting was day-long, the luncheon speaker Logan Wilson, president of the American Council, and the result a determination to explore new avenues for cooperative action. The HEARS plan was put on track. Other ideas would come.[13]

Behind such program movements were changes in the national office, many of them the results of Francis Finn's imaginative approaches to the problems and opportunities before him and his willingness to probe—even to gamble a little—in his search for solutions. The commitments, real or implied—the need for staff, the costs of publications (including a future Administrative Service), the expenses of committee activity that was national in scope—were elements of Finn's own "management challenge." But Finn plunged ahead. The publications program needing relief (Hines still divided between the association and the Committee on Governmental Relations), a new staff member came aboard in September: James K. Blake, a Swarthmore graduate with experience in business publications and college public relations. With the workshops now on a coast-to-coast basis, Sheila Sanjabi the planner and manager, administrative assistance was enlisted there. Still, excepting certain part-time and occasional overload staff, the national programs were being carried on by scarcely more than a dozen persons.

Finn's solutions were in doing what could be done, always with board approval, to keep up the gathering momentum. For special areas of activity there were opportunities for support from appropriate foundations or federal agencies. When the Administrative Service was in early stages, the prospective costs calculable, grants of $25,000 each from the Ford Foundation in 1970 and from the United States Steel Foundation, Inc. in 1971 supported the initial work, the Ford grant to be matched from nondues sources. Another grant from Ford, this for $9,000, helped launch the consultant registry. When the HEARS project was taking shape, a new grant came from Esso. Such assistance was provided, of course, because the association was proving itself a force in the management field and because it presented describable projects of obvious interest to higher education. But pro-

51

jects that could pay their own way did so, if possible. Fees offset most of the costs of the workshops. The workshop manuals and texts were offered for general sale.[14]

The New York meeting that late autumn more than justified all the planning and expectations that had been focused on it. A principal speaker was Roger W. Heyns, president-elect of the American Council, soon to succeed Logan Wilson. Heyns, formerly of the University of Michigan and after 1965 chancellor of the University of California at Berkeley, was equipped to speak with feeling, as he did, about the "Management Challenge." But others did too, among them William J. McGill, president of Columbia; Professor James J. Healy, an industrial relations faculty member at Harvard; William G. Bowen, newly elected president of Princeton; and Samuel Gould, chancellor emeritus of the State University of New York. There was satisfaction in such a convocation, the management theme being so variously addressed. Yet the perplexities of the times showed in the last-minute arrangements for discussions and panel sessions. At a breakfast meeting, business officers held group discussions of such new topics as unemployment compensation, insurance, and personnel-affirmative action policies. A late addition to the schedule was a seminar on implications of the new phase of the wage-price freeze, those implications still not altogether clear. The year had been thus. A challenge.

5

1972-1973: A Time of Proof

THE PERIOD FROM EARLY 1972 to late 1973 was, for the national association, a time of proof. The period began in the puzzles of the wage-price freeze and it ended in the midst of a national crisis, the first gasoline-oil-energy shortage. But the association was demonstrating in the midst of accumulating pressures not only a refreshing flexibility but a kind of daring—a willingness to plunge into efforts to solve problems. The growth of the association kept coming, too. The momentum was real.

The era already was being called "the decade of accountability" in higher education. Troubles on the campuses had focused public attention as never before on the institutions as institutions and on real or presumed shortcomings in their management. If the era was one of perplexity for college and university presidents, it was no less so (and perhaps to a higher degree) for the business officer. Roger Heyns, in his New York talk, had touched on the mood of the time and on what he hoped was the mood in the business office. Of these he said:

> "Business officers are, traditionally and understandably, a realistic group. So all of us are aware of support problems, both financial and emotional. We know that there are serious doubts about the uses of education, serious questions about who should be trained, and how many, and how. These are questions that must be answered. These are also challenging and threatening questions. We can be sure, therefore, that the next decade will be devoted to a great deal of agonizing, soul-searching, self-criticism, and self-renewal.
>
> "This will call for poise on the part of all of us, poise and enterprise, and an overall commitment to make our institutions effective for all their human inhabitants. I hope you all feel, in spite of the severity, a kind of elation about the task."

Heyns's choice of the word "elation" was one that would not have occurred to any in his audience, perhaps. Yet so far as the association was concerned, "elation" was the right word, absolutely apt. There had been extensive coverage of the New York meeting by *The Chronicle of Higher Education,* but the theme reflected in the headline—"Business Officers Seeking a Larger Role in Academic Decisions"—seemed off the point. The business officers' larger role already was theirs by then because they had prepared for it. They had felt elation in the preparation.[1]

In major ways, and in many minor ones, the national association was involved, sometimes at the center, in the new planning, budgeting, costing, resource allocation, and investment management explorations that took the stage in the early years of "the decade of accountability." Planning for the Administrative Service, the new *CUBA*, led off in all directions—first to links between the Accounting Principles Committee and then the AICPA's Committee on College and University Accounting and Auditing, then to each of the association's program committees, then to the appropriate "business-related" groups. But the links within higher education itself, particularly to the American Council, were strong. With the council the association had set up a Higher Education Advisory Committee on problems of the wage-price freeze. With the American Council and the Academy for Educational Development, Inc., the association sponsored in 1972 a working conference on "Confronting the Financial Crisis." With the council and five other organizations the association conducted in Denver a national forum on "New Planning and Management Practices." The council and the association continued to sponsor jointly, year after year, the well-established Institute for College and University Administrators, a five-day study session for business officers and academic deans.* And, of course, business officers were serving on council committees and, as consultants, to the National Center for Higher Education Management Systems at WICHE (NCHEMS), which late in 1972 was ready with a draft of its projected *Higher Education Finance Manual*. In his 1972 report to the membership, Francis Finn noted that the association's opportunity was to make itself a "national resource" in higher education. The association was behaving that way.[2]

---

*Certain leading business officers were otherwise involved, too. There had been established at Harvard by 1970 a new Institute for Educational Management offering an intensive six-week summer course covering the whole field of educational administration, a course once considered highly experimental but proved in practice by 1973 as eminently successful. The national association had no formal connection with the institute, which was located in the Harvard Graduate School of Business Administration, cosponsored by the Graduate School of Education, and funded by foundation and other grants, but business officers helped shape the program from the beginning. Thomas McGoey, while serving in retirement as special consultant to the president of Columbia, became chairman of the IEM board. Among trustees in the formative years were Hertzfeld, Bryant, Conrad, Little, Scheps, and Raymond W. Kettler, State University of New York, and L. Gard Wiggins, Harvard, formerly a member of the Committee on Governmental Relations. Lecturers included Bernard Mintz, City University of New York, and John Meck, Dartmouth.

And the association's growth was, by all measures—in membership, dues income, "outside" support and program activity—remarkable. In *A Profile of NACUBO* published in 1973, the record was set out, in numbers, for the period since 1968, just before the national office moved from 1785 Massachusetts Avenue to One Dupont Circle. The record of five years:

Membership: The totals of institutional members had risen from 970 to 1,417, an increase of 45 percent, the rate unmatched among other higher education associations and established while many were finding memberships static or declining. Institutions with enrollments smaller than 2,000 constituted over 60 percent of the membership—and the number had continued to grow after the dues increase of 1970. In addition to the provisional memberships there now were memberships for associates—nonprofit organizations (libraries, foundations, etc.) with interests in higher education or its management—and regular memberships were available to governing boards administratively responsible for two or more member institutions.

Income and Expenditure: Dues income, at $104,000 in 1968-69, had grown to $300,000, but total income for program purposes was at $689,000 for 1973-74, fees for workshops and other activities bringing $207,000, sales of publications $49,000, and grants and contracts $44,000 for that year alone. Foundation grants since 1970 totaled almost $180,000, and federal support of special programs more than $110,000.

Workshops: Since 1969, when 625 institutional representatives took part in twenty-one workshop sessions, the annual participation had risen by 1973 to 1,600. Institutional representation also had risen each year, from 550 in 1969 to 1,250 in 1973-74.[3]

The 1972 membership meeting—the second annual—was held in Denver on July 9-11, the theme, "Resource Allocation Management in Higher Education," suggesting the particular kinds of thinking then current. The heads of six institutions were there as speakers to provide breadth and background. They were Maurice Mitchell, chancellor of the University of Denver, the "keynoter"; Norman Francis, president of Xavier University; Bruce Heilman, president of the University of Richmond; Malcolm Moos, president of the University of Minnesota; Larry Chalmers, president of the University of Kansas; and Vivian Henderson, president of Clark College. The program was designed by a committee headed by William T. Haywood, who would

55

succeed Harold Myers as president of the association.* Myers, who had been elected in mid-1971, became the only president to preside at two national meetings, but his lengthened term was noteworthy for other reasons, among them the attention that Myers himself gave to encouraging the growth of interassociation coordination and the development of the HEARS program. (It was Myers who also suggested an annual "past presidents' dinner" at national meetings, an idea that led eventually to establishment of a Past Presidents' Advisory Committee.) Serving with Haywood as the new vice president was Robert W. Meyer, Ohio Wesleyan, the secretary, Paul W. Hodson, Utah, and the treasurer, Lester G. Loomis, Brandeis. Five new directors came to the board—five because of interesting and unusual circumstances. Charles C. Teamer of Dillard University took the seat long held by Harold Logan, Tuskegee, who resigned to become a vice president of the Southern Association—the first black to become an officer there. Jesse B. Morgan of Tulane filled the vacancy in the Southern when Haywood became national president and thus under new policy a director-at-large.** Mary Jane Calais of the Junior College District of St. Louis—the first woman director and the first from the junior college field—succeeded Robert Meyer, now also a director-at-large. New from the Eastern Association was Merrill A. Ewing of Mount Holyoke, and from the Western, Robert Gilmore, already deep in national programs as chairman of the Manual Revision Committee. Such were the Denver developments. But what the 1972 meeting proved, the quality of the program everywhere acknowledged, was that the association was capable of conducting only eight months after New York a second meeting national in scope and of more than routine interest to higher education.[4]

Much had happened, naturally, before and after. For one thing, the membership had before it in 1972 the draft of a "Code of Ethics and Standards of Professional Conduct for College and University Business and Financial Officers." Edward Cratsley had been chairman of the drafting committee, his associates C. Russell DeBurlo, Jr., Tufts, and Wilbur Pierpont, Michigan. The statement was distributed for comment, but comments were slow in coming; perhaps this was be-

---

*It was at the Denver meeting that NACUBO honored C. C. DeLong, bursar at the University of Illinois since 1946, for his years of service to the field—more than thirty-five in all—and particularly for his work with the history of the professional organizations. DeLong was given, at the annual dinner on July 10, an Award of Merit recounting his contributions.

**Bylaws amendments approved by member institutions in June 1972 provided (1) that a vice president was the president-elect, thus assuring continuity of service and (2) that board members elected to serve as president or vice president became directors-at-large, the regional associations free to elect replacements.

cause the standards expected—integrity, competence, loyalty, and dedication to institution and profession, avoidance of activity tainted by possible conflicts of interest—were those to which the business officer already adhered. The statement simply was accepted for what it was, a codification of professional standards long honored.[5]

Nothing slowed the workshop studies. To the regular planning-budgeting and fund accounting series had been added by 1972-73 a new series on investment and risk management and insurance. The management continued to be central, Sheila Sanjabi in charge, but course and content were developed by the appropriate committees and the workshops now were cosponsored in each instance by the regional associations. But whereas professional studies thus were strengthened by region, it was the committee work that made all efforts truly national—business officers from coast to coast, from small institutions and large, coming together periodically in their committee meetings to share views and experiences and gain new insights into issues of broad significance. This, too, was a learning process.

The committees were evolving, inevitably, and the leadership changing. The Committee on Plans and Objectives had become the Committee on Goals and Programs, headed first by Robert Meyer, then by Robert Gilmore. W. Harold Read, Tennessee, succeeded Gilbert Lee as chairman of the Accounting Principles Committee. There was by 1973 a Committee on Resource Planning and Management, the chairman Clarence Scheps. With liaison carried to a new height the association committee was a component of the American Council's new Task Force on Resource Assessment, Planning, and Management in Higher Education, Scheps the chairman of that, too. Anthony D. Lazzaro, Southern California, replaced David Baldwin as chairman of the Insurance and Risk Management Committee. The Community Colleges Subcommittee became the Two-Year Colleges Committee, William Cutler still chairman. A. L. Palmer of Howard, then Harvey R. Alexander of Johnson C. Smith, headed the Management at Black Colleges Committee. William Haywood's successors with the Small Colleges Committee were Marwin O. Wrolstad, Lawrence, and A. Dean Buchanan, California Lutheran. Frederick R. Ford, Purdue, who had succeeded Scheps as chairman of the Professional Development Committee, was in turn succeeded by Fred Vorsanger, now at Arkansas. The Taxation Committee was headed successively by Donald E. Blanchard, Knox; John E. Ecklund, Yale; Douglass Hunt, Columbia; and Merl M. Huntsinger, Washington University. Vincent Shea, Virginia, so long chairman of the Publications Committee, was succeeded by Kurt Hertzfeld in 1973, when the Manual Revision Committee merged with the Publications Committee. There were other committees; the total in 1973 was twenty. More than 125 business officers from every region were serving, some on two or more committees with overlapping mandates. If the association was indeed becoming a "national resource," committee work was at the core of it.[6]

At the national office the tooling up in staff and facilities—and in certain refinements of service—went on.

Early in 1972 Steven C. Hychka, who had been assistant contract administrator at Purdue, was brought to Washington to head the HEARS project, the new interassociation Higher Education Administration Referral Service that was being initiated with the help of the two-year $30,000 grant from the Esso Education Foundation. Hychka was a Purdue graduate, his 1967 B.A. degree in industrial management. The project was not really experimental, for its design had been set out clearly in interassociation committee meetings following the original "business-related" group discussions of 1971. Nevertheless, Hychka would be working new ground and he soon was involved also in the conferences that produced the more formal Interassociation Management-Related Group (IMRG).[7]

The expansion of services meant expansions in publications, and these were various. It had been perceived in 1971 that the new flow of writing by business officers included papers that, although valuable, were not at the explorations-of-principle level for which *Professional File* had been designed. The answer had come in development of a new professional series of occasional papers, *Studies in Management,* these also keyed ("Accounting," "Personnel," and so on) for filing. By the end of 1973 twenty issues had appeared. At the same time, because of the rising need for background information from Washington, the NACUBO *Special Reports* were supplemented by NACUBO *Memorandums* carrying timely materials at length. Finally, the new interassociation activity suggested the publication of a quarterly *Professional Calendar* listing in a new format the meetings and workshops of all the business-related organizations and the national and regional associations.* Publication was inaugurated in June 1972.[8]

---

*The Interassociation Management-Related Group, its activities generally coordinated by a committee headed by William Haywood, would include representatives of the National Association of College and University Attorneys, the Campus Safety Association, the International Association of College and University Security Directors, the University Insurance Managers Association, the College and University Systems Exchange, the Association of College Unions—International, the National Association of College and University Food Services, the National Association of Educational Buyers, the National Association of College Auxiliary Services, the Association of College and University Auditors, the Association of College and University Housing Of-

As for staffing, it had been a hope that a "small college specialist" might be added. By 1973 a search was in progress. But not only was the basic publications effort larger, but getting nearer by the month was the time when assistance would be needed for production of the Administrative Service. That process, from the handling of the draft chapters to the design of the total looseleaf product, would require efforts far beyond association experience thus far. Already, however, the Service and the further publication of the single-volume *CUBA* (revised) were being viewed as association projects, the publication rights held so long by the American Council to be transferred, finally, to the association itself. Meanwhile, publications help came, and it came as had happened once before, from within.

G. Richard Biehl, a graduate of Brown (B.A. 1969) and Columbia (M.A. 1971) had come to the association office in 1971 as a temporary employee in a period of overload, a young man working as an expert typist while he awaited another opening in Washington. As it turned out, Biehl stayed, first as an assistant to Blake with *Business Officer,* later with larger assignments in publications. By 1972 he was appointed an information specialist, an entry-level professional position. By late 1973 he was in charge of the development of a new guide, *Federal Regulations and the Employment Practices of Colleges and Universities,* a looseleaf service sponsored by the association with the cooperation of seven other higher education groups.[9]

Growth meant certain adjustments of space. The library was being steadily enlarged, the circulating library was active (some 330 manuals and other materials on loan in 1972-73), and storage was a problem. Yet there was room for another "business-related" office, and soon another. By 1972 the Association of Physical Plant Administrators of Universities and Colleges, its executive director Paul T. Knapp, had joined the College and University Personnel Association as a neighbor in the association's suite. By 1973 the circle was joined by the National Association of College and University Attorneys, Peter L. Wolff the executive director.[10]

Added to the staff, at last, was the "small college specialist," but his responsibility was broader than that and would involve not only extensive committee support but supervision of a new national Information Exchange Service designed to get prompt answers to management questions from member institutions. The specialist was M. J. Williams, former vice president for fiscal affairs and treasurer at Southwestern

ficers, the Association of Physical Plant Administrators of Universities and Colleges, the College and University Personnel Association, the National Association of College Stores, Inc., and the Canadian Association of University Business Officers.

at Memphis. Williams had been active in the small-college field and he brought that experience to the office. He worked with the Personnel Committee and other committees as well as with the Small Colleges Committee. A month after his arrival in August 1973, Williams was setting up the new information service.[11]

There emerged in this time a program that, originating in the black college management-improvement effort, proved in the end to have benefits for institutions throughout higher education. It was, in addition, a significant early sample of interassociation coordination.

In 1972 the association had applied for and received, through the U.S. Office of Education, an Education Professions Development Act grant of $35,000 to support an institute in physical plant management, a project conceived as of specific assistance to the black colleges and to be sponsored cooperatively with APPA, the association's new neighbor. By autumn the program had been designed in consultations involving Paul Knapp and other APPA representatives (among them Ted B. Simon, Michigan State, and George O. Weber, Maryland) and members of the association's Management at Black Colleges Committee, then headed by A.L. Palmer, Howard. For the study session APPA developed a workbook, *Physical Plant Management for Small Schools,* and when the institute was held in New Orleans in October more than seventy administrators of black colleges were present, by invitation, the effort widely regarded as a thoroughly successful entry into a new realm of cooperative professional service. Successful it was, but the success did not end there. Not only were the benefits cumulative, but from the program had come by 1974 a new and expanded text, *A Basic Manual for Physical Plant Administration,* written by Weber and published jointly by APPA and the association.[12]

The annual meeting of 1973 was held July 8-10 at Chicago's Conrad Hilton Hotel. The program (with Lloyd Goggin of Miami University as chairman) was built about the theme, "The Dynamics of Higher Education." On a long list of principal speakers and panel leaders were the names of Kingman Brewster, president of Yale; Glenn Dumke, chancellor of the California State University and Colleges; Father James T. Burtchaell, provost of the University of Notre Dame; Ernest L. Boyer, chancellor of the State University of New York; Jean Allard, vice president for business and finance, Chicago; and Bernice Sandler, director of the Project on the Status of Women in the Association of American Colleges. From wherever came the "Dynamics" theme, the year was for the association a year of that dynamic kind—a year of preparation for, among other things, assuming full responsibility for development, design, and publication of the Administrative

60

Service as a prelude to the revised *College and University Business Administration.* [13]

Staffing for the Service effort was completed as 1973 began. Director of the *CUBA* revision was Abbott Wainwright, and the administrative secretary was Lanora F. Welzenbach. Each had experience the occasion required. Wainwright, a graduate of the University of Miami (B.A. 1957, M.B.A. 1968), had editorial experience with corporate and federal programs, and came to the association from a private firm serving business clients in the field of employee benefit programs. He was, in addition, an instructor in finance in the evening programs of the University of Baltimore's School of Business. Welzenbach was an experienced editor and writer (some of her writing published in England) with no business office experience but with capabilities for adaptability and learning. Long before the 1973 membership meeting, work on the Administrative Service by staff and committees was under way. [14]

Adaptability and willingness to learn were required of all hands that year, business officers in the field not excluded. Every program committee and most of the related associations would be involved in the Administrative Service mobilization. Back of it all was an association-wide involvement in the drafting and ultimate approval of the AICPA committee's new guide, *Audits of Colleges and Universities.* A National Commission on the Financing of Postsecondary Education, created by Congress in 1972, now was staffed and turning to the association, among many higher education groups, for consultation. On such multiplying demands for services and counsel the national board kept a somewhat nervous eye—nervous, at least so far as a pending major membership decision was concerned. The board had approved a proposal for a dues increase considered essential to assure proper support of activities for the next five to seven years. The answer, in the usual national referendum, would come in 1973. On it, much would depend. Robert Meyer was national president, Robert Gilmore vice president (and designated successor), the secretary Merrill Ewing, and the treasurer Jesse Morgan. New directors were Lloyd Goggin; Paul Linfield, Franklin and Marshall; Roger D. Lowe, Wichita State; Donald Marburg, Beloit; and H. S. Thomson, Washington.

The proposed dues structure had been thoroughly studied in board and committee meetings. It departed from the outmoded system of basing dues solely on the enrollments of member institutions. Instead, the new schedule asked dues based on both enrollments and current fund expenditures. The schedule was complex. It would mean increased payments by all institutions, although for the colleges that formed so much of the membership the increases would be modest. A difficulty was that the schedule needed to be explained, and explained in connection with the association's projected needs for funds to support the new services. Through 1973 the proposal was discussed in regional association meetings, the board finally altering the plan to permit a two-year implementation. Still, none could be certain that the 1,417 member institutions—some of them new—would produce a majority favoring increase. But late that year they did. By September 1973, when the mail ballots were counted, the vote was not heavy (many institutions abstained), but the majority was overwhelming. The proposal was approved and the first of the two annual increases would be effective in fiscal 1974-75.[15]

The preparation and eventual publication of the AICPA's *Audits of Colleges and Universities* was, in a way, an effort timed fortuitously to become a warm-up for heavy work with the Administrative Service. The AICPA committee, in being for several years, was headed in 1971-72 by Daniel D. Robinson, of Peat, Marwick, Mitchell & Co., who was pressing forward the development of exposure drafts of the new audit guide. Robinson and his associates (other long-term committee members including Delford W. Edens, of Haskins & Sells, and Jay H. Anderson, of Price Waterhouse & Co.) were in touch with association thinking, for an early contact had been established with the Accounting Principles Committee during Gilbert Lee's chairmanship, and Scheps and Gilmore had been designated the association's liaison representatives to the AICPA group. Recent consultations had proceeded expeditiously and Robinson had anticipated release of the exposure drafts by mid-1972. Not until autumn, however, were the drafts ready for the wider review, and it was then that the association—with Harold Read and his Accounting Principles Committee colleagues leading the way—mobilized a series of regional meetings from which the business officers' responses emerged. In October 1972, with the exposure drafts now in the field, each regional association president was asked to appoint a panel of forty business officers considered most knowledgeable in accounting and familiar with the issues involved. In a set of regional seminars then scheduled by the association, the business officer panelists met with representatives of the AICPA and Accounting Principles Committee, Read, Scheps, and Gilmore participating in selected sessions. The responses from these meetings were sifted by the Accounting Principles Committee and put into a draft response presented by Read for approval by the association board in December 1972. The board approved a set of sixteen proposed changes—fourteen of which were accepted immediately by the AICPA committee—and in its deliberations the board had the views not only of Read, Scheps, and Gilmore, but of two Accounting

Principles Committee veterans, Norman H. Gross, California, and Harold E. Bell, Chicago, and of John Dozier, Macalester, now chairman of the Investment Committee. When copies of the audit guide became available in August 1973, the association made a distribution to member institutions. So close had been the association's interest in the work, and so general the participation, that the guide was being considered the association's own statement until pertinent new chapters of the Administrative Service were ready for release.[16]

And draft chapters were coming. The Service and the follow-on volumes of *CUBA* now definitely would be the association's own, the publication rights having been released by the American Council. The association could experience mixtures of anxiety and pride as work proceeded, for the project was of a kind unprecedented in higher education—light years away from the *Financial Reports* of the prefederation 1930s and 1940s. The process of drafting and approval was carefully measured: (1) a field of professional interest was identified; (2) basic drafts of revisions or new materials were prepared; (3) manuscripts were submitted for professional review; (4) drafts were further reviewed for technical accuracy by committee members or outside consultants; (5) the drafts as edited were circulated for additional comment; (6) drafts went to a final, general readership; and (7) the chapters were approved for release by the association board. No such precision ever had been expected before. But by autumn 1973 the Administrative Service had been designed, the production costs calculated, the subscription plan and fees decided, and the association's publication intentions announced. With the AICPA guide now in circulation and filling the gap, the chapters on accounting and auditing would not be expected before spring 1974.[17]

The larger movements had been proceeding, meantime—at NCHEMS and in the offices of the National Commission on the Financing of Higher Education—with the continuing attention of Francis Finn and members of the relevant committees. The association itself, with the help of Ford Foundation awards totaling $89,100, was sponsoring an accounting research project and investment-performance studies. There was a new Joint Accounting Group (JAG), its mission to bring together the thinking of the association, AICPA, and NCHEMS in development of a common terminology, with definitions, applicable to all higher educational institutions. The Joint Accounting Group did indeed develop a terminology agreed to by each of the three organizations, the terminology thus adopted, perforce, in the NCHEMS *Higher Education Finance Manual* and in the federal Higher Education General Information Survey (HEGIS) materials. Meantime, the Committee on Governmental Relations was continuingly active—Linda Wilson the chairman after June 1973 and Howard Wile long since a highly respected presence in the realm of government-university relations. To the association's lengthening list of manuals and workbooks had been added that year a text of singular timeliness, *Risk Management and Insurance: Guidelines for Higher Education,* the author John F. Adams, of Georgia State, and still a principal in committee affairs. But hovering over all was the feeling that publication of the revised *CUBA,* initiated through the new Administrative Service, would be an event of epochal importance—to higher education in general, and to business officers in particular.[18]

It would be so. But there had come unexpectedly that autumn a set of problems completely apart from those that had been drawing attention for so long. The national shortage of oil and gasoline had arrived, and the colleges were hit hard in many ways, from the simple absence of heating oil to the need to try to anticipate the inevitably higher costs of operations. The situation was one of crisis, and the association, the American Council, and the other educational agencies would be dealing with it for awhile, the ultimate solutions not clear. In December, after a wide survey of institutional problems, *Business Officer* published a roundup report headed "Energy and the Campus: A Time for Plans, Hard Decisions." An early hint of the truth, certainly—and a glimpse of what was coming in 1974.[19]

But did anyone now wonder—after all that had happened—about the business officer's professionalism? Business officers had asked questions of themselves in the first place. Were there answers?

Three doctoral dissertations of 1973 were devoted to the business officer, studies at St. Norbert and Purdue presenting profiles of the chief business officer of the "large" institution, another at Florida State, based on a sampling at land-grant institutions, concerned with the business officer's own view of the role. The conclusions could not be fairly capsuled, of course, but certain findings were noteworthy. The St. Norbert study (the sample 103, nationwide) found that 30 percent of the respondents held master-level degrees, almost 25 percent doctoral. Substantial fractions of the advanced work were in educational administration. The Purdue inquiry (the initial sample at ninety-nine public institutions) found that while the chief business officer usually was selected for experience, he or she was characteristically the recognized expert in financial affairs and, as a member of the administrative team, on the same organizational level as the chief academic officer. Those in the position tended to feel that they had reached their career goal. But how did they view themselves in their role? What, as the Florida State study asked, were their satisfactions or dissatisfactions? Here such difficult-to-quantify elements as idealism, prestige, and self-fulfillment were present, yet from the survey interesting impressions emerged. Business officers were restless if they felt their job limited to helping accomplish, rather than helping define, their institution's goals. But they experienced a high degree of satisfaction in their work and, revealingly, attached importance "to being able to give help to other people. . . ." Perhaps that was the truly professional answer.[20]

And perhaps it was indicative of the business officers' stature that their own institutions were honoring them in permanent ways. At Purdue, in 1972, the university's Memorial Center was renamed the Stewart Center in acknowledgment of the services of R. B. Stewart—the association's Bob Stewart—a Purdue administrator from 1925 until his retirement in 1961. In that year, too, the University of Houston's Graduate Studies Building became Charles F. McElhinney Hall in honor of the "Mr. Mac" who had served the institution since 1934, in later years as vice president (and once as acting president) and finally as senior vice president and treasurer, the position he still held. McElhinney, no less than Stewart, had been one of the leading spirits in the long movement of business officers into association and to whatever professional position they had achieved. Vincent Shea, who had been with the University of Virginia since 1936, and since 1970 its vice president, received in 1974 the university's Thomas Jefferson award, its highest honor for service. When Harry L. Baker, Jr. died suddenly in 1973, Georgia Tech dedicated a building to his memory. Baker had served his institution as research administrator and, for a decade, the association, with the Committee on Governmental Relations.[21]

6

1974-1979: The Theme—Management

IT WAS EASY, EVEN AT THE TIME, to see the year 1974 as one marking the opening of a significant phase of the national association's movement toward true maturity. The year began with publication, through the new Administrative Service, of the first dozen chapters of *College and University Business Administration* (1974), that refinement of an idea originally realized in publication of "Volumes I and II" almost a quarter of a century earlier. The new *CUBA* was the association's own now, a perpetual commitment to the delineation of sound management practice throughout higher education. But the launching took place at a moment in which the association, if it were to fulfill its obligations, had to be responsive in fields undreamed of in the 1950s and in which higher education needed not just statements of management principle, but immediate management help in the way of instant information, informed judgments, quick consensus. Energy problems were blossoming, a new Federal Energy Office publishing mandatory fuel allocation regulations. The National Commission on the Financing of Postsecondary Education was calling for "national standard procedures" to make financial information more readily available. The Cost of Living Council still was issuing wage-price guidelines affecting colleges and universities. The Environmental Protection Agency, the Equal Employment Opportunity Commission, and the Occupational Safety and Health Administration were similarly busy. From whatever direction the problems and questions were coming, college and university management was affected and the national association deeply involved.[1]

More than 2,400 sets of Administrative Service materials—the *CUBA* chapters and introductory sections in looseleaf binders—were mailed in January 1974. But the first set had been presented by President Robert W. Meyer to Roger Heyns, president of the American Council, during a council board meeting on January 22. Heyns had written for the Service a short foreword in which he recalled the historic links between the council and the business officers during the

CUBA development and emphasized the continuing need for such an instrument under the aegis of the association. He wrote:

> "Publication of this revision . . . carries forward into a new time, and in an entirely new way, an effort that has been of singular significance to higher education and one that the American Council on Education views with understandable satisfaction.
>
> "This revision is addressed to a new era in higher education management and to a future that certainly will bring more changes than we now can see. Yet the authority . . . springs from a most interesting past in which certain dedicated college and university business officers, for whose vision and initiative we still are grateful, developed studies of management principle that were published by the American Council. . . .
>
> "With this volume the American Council on Education now transfers to the National Association a responsibility in which the Council will continue to have a large interest. . . . The times call for a professional reference devoted to management principles; the member institutions of the Council will look to the new *College and University Business Administration* for guidance in this important field."[2]

The word was management. It was a word about which themes would be built, as was the theme of the 1974 national meeting to be held in Boston: "Management and Financing of Higher Education."

The association's task in the period beginning in 1974 was to position itself most usefully in a changing higher education landscape, keeping its basic programs moving smoothly while it sorted out and assigned priorities to new demands for service. The national board discussed such questions repeatedly. The Goals and Programs Committee was active, first under vice president Robert Gilmore in 1973-74 and then, when Gilmore moved to the presidency, under vice president Merrill Ewing. The association's financial status was strong. The dues alone, under the new schedule, would bring $600,000 in 1975 and total revenues would reach $1,294,000. The programs-in-being were proving wonderfully successful. Workshops were more than paying their own way—income from workshops and meetings at $300,000 by 1975—and sales of books were helping to offset the costs of the publications-information program. The Administrative Service had been welcomed and, almost simultaneously, it was joined by another looseleaf subscription service, *Federal Regulations and the Employment Practices of Colleges and Universities,* launched by the association with the joint sponsorship of seven other higher education organizations and designed to meet new needs for information in relation to affirmative action, civil rights, and fair employment legislation. By 1974 the HEARS project, initiated with the help of an Esso grant, was in its second successful year, already meeting most of its operating costs (more than 425 positions were listed). HEARS was the centerpiece of the increasingly meaningful Interassociation Management-Related Group effort, but other projects were in the works—an expanded and refined *Professional Calendar,* a publishable *Profile* of the IMRG member organizations (histories, structures, missions), and new series of jointly sponsored workshops or seminars on questions of mutual interest, such as the new OSHA requirements. New vistas kept opening—some presenting opportunities, some obligations—and the energy situation was among the most important. The problem was that each prospect for such new service suggested program or staff adjustments of some kind or changes in the association's management or committee structure. Francis Finn was being imaginative in many ways—in enlisting federal or foundation support for special projects, in encouraging flexibility in every part of the national office operation, from staff support to use of space—but decision as to direction rested ultimately with the national board. Hence the repeated board discussions; hence the consultative ministrations of the Goals and Programs Committee.[3]

Gilmore was national president for 1974-75, the vice president Ewing, the secretary Roger Lowe, Wichita State, and the treasurer Jesse Morgan, Tulane. The new team had taken over at the July 10-12 meeting at Boston's Statler Hilton Hotel (Lowe the program chairman), the discussions focused on the possible effect of the recent National Postsecondary Commission report and the keynote speaker President Richard W. Lyman, of Stanford. When Ewing became national president in 1975, at the national meeting in New Orleans, he would head the continuing studies of program choices until he passed the responsibility to Jesse Morgan at the 1976 meeting—held in Washington, appropriately, in the nation's bicentennial year—the management theme again in view, this time, "Performance Management: Staying on Top of the Job." Serving with Morgan were Reuben H. Lorenz, Wisconsin, vice president; John F. Zeller, Bucknell, secretary; and A. Dean Buchanan, California Lutheran, treasurer. By 1977, when the national meeting was in San Francisco, Lorenz was president, the vice president Anthony D. Lazzaro, Southern California; the secretary Mary M. Lai, Long Island University; and the treasurer Orie E. Myers, Jr., of Emory. By this time a number of critical rearrangements of staff and modes of operation had occurred and certain significant new projects had been set on course.

It was not surprising that the energy situation of 1973-74 had brought responses, for the association's obligations were formidable even though they were shared with the American Council, the Association of Physical Plant Administrators, and others. The surprise, if any, was in the variety of projects that the association sustained even in a period of staff change and necessary growth. What was happening, between 1974 and 1977, at the national office?

The national office staff never had been large. But like the American Council, it served institutions of all kinds (even the "emerging" institutions), plus growing numbers of associated commissions, foundations, and libraries and, particularly with its Administrative Service, the "subscriber" organizations. The membership was growing by the month. The basic membership of 1,417 in 1974 had risen to 1,730 in 1977 (by which time it was larger than the membership of the American Council), the regional distribution thus: Eastern, 485; Central, 456; Southern, 562; and Western, 227. The membership lists included institutions outside the United States, from Canada to France, Lebanon, and Saudi Arabia. The association's appeal lay in its basic activities—instruction in well-planned workshops, studies by committees of management questions and techniques, and dissemination of information through publications. The strength was in the regional association composition and in the use of committees to attack national problems, but every problem, project, or interassociation activity required staff attention, support, or coordination. Thus while the national staff was larger than some others in actual numbers, it was no larger than it had to be to do what was expected of it. If the staff were to keep up with new demands for service, growth was indicated. But growth came a step at a time.[4]

On the governmental relations front, Howard Wile continued in 1974 to represent the committee and the association with an expertness well honed by a decade in Washington. In publications-information were Neal Hines (soon to retire); G. Richard Biehl, now editor of *Business Officer* and also developing, almost single-handedly, the new *Employment Practices* series; Abbott Wainwright, editor of the Administrative Service, with Lanora Welzenbach the staff assistant there; and Rachael Lowder, a new publications staff member. The workshops and meetings—including the national meetings, which now required almost year-around planning—continued to be the responsibility of Sheila Sanjabi, director of professional programs. Steven Hychka, managing HEARS and staffing half a dozen program committees, also was naturally at the center of the interassociation activity, and M.J. Williams, as director of special programs, was serving the two-year college field (including helping with the development of a new small-college personnel management guide) while coordinating the Information Exchange Service.

Many staff members helped serve the national committees by arranging meetings, preparing agenda, acting as recorders, and preparing reports; they also helped maintain appropriate liaison with the regional associations. With the staff, as with so many of the programs, flexibility was the rule, and the most interesting circumstance was that the staff as a whole represented only a modicum of actual experience in a college or university business office. The staff, growing in their assignments, were serving the professionals who served the profession, but they knew the institutions, the people, the needs, the views. They were generalists in specialized ways, and they developed an *esprit* of their own. The staff changes that came after 1974 were in part simply evolutionary, but most were responses to the new times.

When Hines retired in 1974, his seven years with the association acknowledged during the national meeting in Boston, he was succeeded by Biehl, and in the subsequent staff adjustments Rachael Lowder became briefly the editor of *Business Officer* until she was made manager of general services (including personnel) and Jeffrey M. Sheppard joined the staff as editor.* Sheppard, a graduate of George Washington University, worked as a newspaper reporter and congressional aide prior to joining the staff as editor of *Business Officer*. But the era was bringing pressures in dozens of new ways—all requiring staff and information activity—most flowing from federal legislation or regulation in areas from copyright law to taxation, safety and health rules, and personnel practices including collective bargaining, affirmative action, and retirement. Such questions were apart from those within the purview of the Committee on Governmental Relations, oriented historically to issues of primary interest to the research institutions, and thus by 1975 the association had created a new functional area called Federal Focus, and Hychka was put in charge of this.

---

*Upon Hines's departure the national board established, with the help of contributions from a number of members, a Neal O. Hines Publications Award to be presented annually to persons whose professional writings or other publications activities were considered most significant. The program was inaugurated at the 1976 Washington meeting, when awards went to three winners: John F. Adams, Georgia State; E.E. Davidson, Oklahoma State; and Norman H. Gross, California. Winners in subsequent years were: 1977, Kurt M. Hertzfeld, Amherst, and J. Leslie Hicks, Jr., Denison; 1978, Raymond J. Woodrow, Princeton; 1979, Max A. Binkley, Colorado State; 1980, Dean H. Kelsey, Albright; and 1981, William M. Wilkinson, Rochester. Two of the winners were authors of books published by NACUBO—Adams, with *Risk Management and Insurance: Guidelines for Higher Education,* and Woodrow, with *Management for Research in U.S. Universities.* Others had done outstanding work in the revision of *CUBA,* in the preparation of other books, in contributing papers, or in review of manuscripts of articles and books.

Succeeding Hychka with HEARS was Charles M. Cochran, Jr., a graduate of Albion with an M.B.A. from Northeastern, who took over a program which then had seventeen interassociation sponsors, including the American Council, and which before long would have two more. (Cochran's father became a college business officer, as did his grandfather, who was a president of the Eastern Association and served on the first federation board.) But demands for information services, including information gathering, were far from satisfied. It was but one of several long-term developments that the association's Costing Standards Committee, headed by John L. Green, Jr., University of Miami, was working with the NCHEMS group on a new instructional manual (Technical Report No. 65) implementing the NCHEMS Information Exchange Procedures project initiated in 1972. By late 1976 the association had added a staff member, a financial analyst, whose first task would be to become the Costing Standards Committee-NCHEMS link, and the new man was K. Scott Hughes, most recently a director of administrative records at Stanford, but a graduate of Illinois (B.S. and M.S. in accounting science) and a C.P.A. with experience in accounting systems design. Before 1976 was out, Wainwright had been made associate director of information and publications and Welzenbach had succeeded him as editor of the Administrative Service. Changes came, and growth, and some of the growth was, appropriately, from within, as when young people who had come to the staff as secretaries or assistants moved up to larger responsibilities, among them Linda Johnston, staff associate for professional programs.[5]

And it was in 1976, eleven years after he had taken Nelson Wahlstrom's place in the old Committee on Governmental Relations office at 1785 Massachusetts Avenue, that Howard Wile retired. It was only one of Wile's achievements that he had held the committee's central functions on an unwavering course while the sponsoring association was getting its bearings, defining its own missions, and organizing for what proved to be years of rocketing growth. Wile had kept in view the committee's special identity—its essential separateness in origin, history, mission, and support—while never failing to participate fully in association meetings or committee or information activities in which his experience was needed. His judgment had been of that kind throughout. He and the knowledge he brought were welcomed in the federal agencies, where he had won respect and trust in years of participation, usually alone, in uncountable numbers of conferences in which resolution of government-university issues frequently depended simply on adjustments of language in policy or regulation. Wile was familiar to many of the federal departmental executives and

71

policy makers, and many of these had been guests and speakers at the committee's meetings, regular or annual. But in the discussions of questions important to the institutions—and there were ninety-eight supporting institutions in 1976—the federal agencies always knew that Wile represented a committee that represented the higher education side. Wile's style throughout had been his own, a mix of deep experience, skill with words, interests that ranged far beyond the demands of his office, and, above all, a quick sense of humor.

When it came to selecting Wile's successor, the choice was Reagan A. Scurlock, of Pennsylvania, who was finishing his second three-year term with the committee. Scurlock, a World War II combat pilot with a J.D. degree from the University of Texas Law School, was familiar with sponsored-research problems from both the federal and the university points of view. Before going to Pennsylvania in 1968 as director of research administration, he had served the U.S. Air Force for eight years as chief of its major contract and procurement policy offices and, finally, as chairman of the Armed Services Procurement Regulation Committee of the Department of Defense. He recently had compiled a comprehensive manual, *Government Contracts and Grants for Research: A Guide for Colleges and Universities,* a work undertaken with support by the National Science Foundation's Management Improvement Program and published by the association in 1975.[7]

For his first months in office Scurlock had the assistance of Dorothy Kolinsky, who had served with Wile since 1965, but by the end of the year she too had retired, her experience—and her spirit—much missed and her final contribution the preparation of a thirty-page set of procedural guidelines for her position. Soon Scurlock had a new assistant executive director, Milton Goldberg, since 1969 director of grants and contracts at Maryland, who already had worked on special projects for the national office.[8]

Certain of the association's major projects of the 1970s were, as with the costing studies, technical in nature and of promise as offering necessary future refinements in management practice. Some, although perhaps no less technical, represented mobilizations of institutional ideas in fields of immediate and critical concern. These tended by their nature to be highly visible. One was the Energy Task Force. Another was the Cost Reduction Incentive Awards Program.

The Energy Task Force had evolved from the initial efforts by the association and the Association of Physical Plant Administrators to grapple with the crisis that struck the institutions in 1973-1974. The association had immediately called for energy-saving ideas, publishing two *Special Reports* on Federal Energy Office requirements, and

APPA's Paul Knapp, with the cooperation of the association and the American Council, had prepared an *Energy Conservation Checklist* sent to all member institutions. It was clear, however, that mere exchanges of information were not enough—academic schedules as well as institutional budgets were affected—and that long-term approaches, probably including research, energy audits, workshops, and publication of technical manuals, would be necessary. The program would be costly. But by 1975 an organization was in being.

The task force was jointly sponsored by the association, APPA, and the American Council. Its office was established initially at Yale, with David Newton as executive director, John Embersits, Yale's energy advisor, as head of the steering group, and John P. Moran, of Princeton, as chairman of a program development committee charged with devising an educational program incorporating workshops and publications. The cost of a three-year effort was estimated at $900,000. In the autumn of 1975 a grant of $100,000 came from the Exxon Corporation, and in January 1977, Exxon's board approved (as the energy crisis deepened) another grant in the same amount. Task force planning proceeded. By November 1977, a third Exxon $100,000 grant had been received, and additional support was coming from other corporations and federal agencies ($75,000 from the Federal Energy Administration to support the workshops, $7,500 from the IBM Corporation, and so on). With the machinery in motion, the central task force office was moved in 1977 to the association's headquarters in Washington, and Steven Hychka, still managing the Federal Focus project, was put in charge.[9]

Thus it was that by 1976 the efforts to assist higher education institutions in the energy field were firmly in place, national in scope, and accelerating. Regular and extensive reports on federal actions and institutional experience were appearing in *Business Officer* and in the APPA and American Council newsletters. A national higher education energy cost and consumption survey, initiated under the auspices of the council's Higher Education Panel—a survey developed by the task force in consultation with the FEA and the U.S. Office of Education—soon produced statistical information that was reported to all institutions. The association, so experienced in the workshop field, was in charge of the new series of energy seminars for business officers and physical plant directors, the first set of nine sessions conducted coast-to-coast in autumn 1976, others to follow. Information supplied by the task force was used by congressional committees considering the effect on higher education of new and proposed energy legislation. The task force maintained a continuing liaison with the Energy Research and Development Administration, the Department of Housing and Urban Development, and the Department of Health, Education, and Welfare, each an agency involved in policy formulation. By 1977 the association had published a comprehensive manual, *Energy Management for Colleges and Universities,* prepared by the task force and incorporating in appendixes case-study materials from representative institutions. Along lines such as these the task force was ready to deal, at both general and technical levels, with energy issues which all agreed would not fade away. By 1979 Exxon support alone totaled $545,000.[10]

The association's Cost Reduction Incentive Awards Program was related to the exigencies of the energy situation, but perhaps even more explicitly, to the inflation-recession pressures that all institutions were feeling in the 1970s. (A 1975 survey by the American Council found "massive evidence of widespread retrenchment in higher education," 34 percent of the private institutions and 16 percent of the public reporting deficits for the most recent fiscal year.) The result, in any case, was that the association conceived and shaped a cost-reduction-idea program to reward, with unrestricted grants ranging from $500 to $10,000, institutional ingenuity in saving. The program was launched in 1975 with a $70,000 grant from the U.S. Steel Foundation and was continued in subsequent years with regular U.S. Steel awards.* The new ideas thus generated were impressive in their variety and the numbers of winners of cash or honorable mention awards eventually were in the hundreds.[11]

There were other programs—sponsored programs—whose objectives were expanding the association's service areas. The Ford Foundation, which had awarded almost $100,000 for accounting and investment projects in 1973, later added $12,400 for revision of the *College Operating Manual,* $47,650 for development of a nontraditional costing model, and $15,750 for an accounting procedures training manual for women administrators. IBM, supporting the Energy Task Force, also granted $8,000 for evaluation of a cost analysis manual. In early 1977 the association began, with the Association of Governing

---

Newsweek magazine considered the program worth a note, its 1976 report beginning, "Colleges compete on almost every conceivable level, so in these hard times it seems natural that they vie for the best way to cut costs." (*Newsweek,* Aug. 9, 1976)

Caltech, with a "phantom tube" lighting device, was the winner of the first $10,000 cost-reduction prize. First-place winners in following years were: 1977, Lane Community College, Eugene, Ore. (energy conservation system); 1978, Creighton University ("creative improvement" program); 1979, Daytona Beach Community College ("energy conservation applications" program); 1980, Skidmore College (alternative fuel from waste motor oil); and 1981, Gonzaga University (new shower-stall repair technique). In 1981 NACUBO published a booklet containing summaries of all cost-reduction ideas that had won cash awards during the first five years of the program.

74

Boards of Universities and Colleges, a two-year project seeking to determine the kinds of information needed by trustees in the management of institutional finances. The cost of this would be $177,000, basic funding coming in a $138,000 grant from the W.K. Kellogg Foundation. But among the projects was one that was the business officers' own—a professional leave program enabling the financial administrator to get away from the office and pursue an activity advancing professional growth.[12]

The Administrative Leave Program was funded by the Exxon Education Foundation, a grant of $61,500 in 1975 followed by another of $35,000 the next year. The program would have been an astonishment to those early business officers whose opportunities for personal growth had been necessarily so self-supported.* Awards ranging from $3,000 to $5,000 were made available to business officers whose project proposals were considered most relevant and whose institutions were prepared to release them temporarily at full salary. Thirteen $3,000 awards were made the first year, 1976—the recommendations by a committee of business officers serving without compensation— seven awards of $4,000 the next year, and thirteen of $5,000 for 1978. The projects thus supported covered a wide spectrum of management interests—investment performance, personnel development, energy conservation, planning systems—and all projects were reported in abstracts for the information of member institutions.** It was a measure of professional progress over the years that many of the winning proposals came from business officers of small colleges, including the black colleges, administrators who in former times would have had no chance at all for such revitalizing experiences.[13]

In 1976, shortly before the bicentennial-year meeting in Washington, D.C., the magazine *Change* published an article on the national association, its history, and its projects. The article was in feature-story style (the somewhat irreverent title, "Nuts-and-Bolts Aid for the Money Men"), but its central point was clear: in times that were difficult for higher education, the association's services were very welcome. The article closed with this paragraph:

---

*Some, but not all, of the pioneers had lived to see the national association in the years of its expansion as a professional organization. Lloyd Morey had died in the *CUBA* revision period (1965), George Van Dyke in 1970, and Nelson Wahlstrom in 1972. Harvey Cain was 86 when he died in February 1974, and Irwin K. (Ike) French, president of the national federation in 1953-55, died in April 1977.

**One early product of the program was a book published by NACUBO in 1977, *Cash Management and Short-Term Investments for Colleges and Universities,* its author Leonard H. Haag, of Ferris State College, Michigan, one of the award winners in 1975-76.

"NACUBO's successes may inspire other organizations, beset by complaining and resigning members. For the future, it will probably continue to grow, though perhaps more slowly than before. But an increase in size may bring a decrease in responsive and efficient management. Then NACUBO will have to determine priorities and define its role more carefully. For the present, however, what its members want is the same—and more of it."[14]

As a prediction, the summary came to seem a good try, only partly right. The membership continued to grow, from 1,650 in 1976 to 1,760 in 1978 and 1,873 by mid-1979. There were adjustments in staff and committee structure in this time, and even another dues increase, but nothing suggested a slowing of responsiveness because of the association's larger size. And as for refining priorities and defining its role, the association simply was setting a course for the rest of the decade.

It was of more than passing importance that the association was by this time a member of the Washington Higher Education Secretariat, an organization of seventeen associations having Washington headquarters, representatives meeting regularly to discuss issues of common concern. The significance was that the Secretariat (the American Council's Roger Heyns was chairman) determined, when the need arose, which association would become the "chosen instrument," authorized to speak for all with regard to a specific issue affecting higher education. Francis Finn was the association's representative, and the association itself was, increasingly, the "chosen instrument" in areas of management. A somewhat special case was in what was known as the HEATH (Higher Education and the Handicapped) project, an American Council effort to which the association would make a significant contribution.

The HEATH development was the response within higher education to the requirements set out in section 504 of the Rehabilitation Act of 1973, which mandated equal access by qualified handicapped persons to all educational activities receiving federal support. The section 504 regulations had been published in mid-1977 by HEW's Office for Civil Rights, which administered the program and which had established deadlines for implementation, including institutional self-evaluations. The implications were sweeping—on the typical campus virtually every office would be involved—and thus the American Council, to assist institutions at large, organized HEATH and was awarded a $100,000 contract by the Department of Health, Education, and Welfare to mobilize an information and assistance effort. Four associations, including APPA, CUPA, and NEXUS (with the general support of fifteen other organizations), would be performing

HEATH work under subcontracts with the council. The association's assignment was the preparation of an extensive manual on institutional self-evaluation. By January 1978, the manual was published as the *Guide to the Section 504 Self-Evaluation for Colleges and Universities,* a 125-page handbook for which Biehl had been coordinator, author, designer, and editor. The course of section 504 developments would be monitored for months thereafter by an association task force operating within the interassociation HEATH organization.[15]

Growth brought changes, naturally, not only in staff (which never seemed as large as the multiple tasks it handled), but in rearrangements of space in the national office, where the original conference room long since had given way to new typing-station desks and work areas, where the library was expanding, and where additional cabinets and tables were required for bulk storage, mailing, photocopying, and so on. Early in 1977 Paul Knapp's APPA office had moved from the association's suite to Eleven Dupont Circle, that space freed for the association's publications work; and to further ease the pressures of mailing and storage, new accommodations were found on the first floor of the National Center building. If any of this suggested that, as *Change* had hinted, growth would inhibit responsiveness, the case would have been difficult to prove, although revisions in staff assignments had to be made.

By April 1977, Charles Cochran, under whose direction HEARS continued to be successful, was named business manager, but to stay with HEARS until a successor was found. Cochran thus assumed responsibility for the association's accounting, budgeting, investments, and general office functions including personnel, which had been left without assignment with the resignation of Rachael Lowder a month earlier. (Lowder had entered another field, but in her four years with the association she had made valuable contributions to publications and, finally, to personnel, where she had regularized and improved employment procedures.) Succeeding Cochran at HEARS in July 1977 was Peter G. Hunt, a graduate of New Hampshire (B.S., business management) and George Washington (M.S., education), recently a manager in private industry. Hunt had been with HEARS all the way: he had found the position as a HEARS registrant.[16]

Perhaps the most visible of the changes was in *Business Officer,* which became a newsmagazine. The move was in a way flexibility in reverse, for it represented a consolidation in the information-professional publication effort. Yet the plans drafted by Jeffrey Sheppard had an inescapable logic, for consolidation itself was by now an act of flexibility. The idea was discussed for a year by the Publications Committee (the chairman was Robert L. Carr, of the Office of the Council of State

College and University Presidents, State of Washington) and approved by the national board in April 1977. The first issue appeared the following September.

Business Officer, under a succession of editors, had become in eleven years a news publication widely recognized in higher education, its reports of Washington developments shared by business officers with their presidents and staffs, its news of association activities welcomed. *Business Officer* had begun modestly, but since 1972 it had been published twelve times a year (the demand for information permitting no summer break), and its basic eight pages had been supplemented by a quarterly *Professional Calendar* and regular *In NACUBO* inserts in which association news was covered by Lanora Welzenbach. By 1977 *Business Officer's* monthly circulation was about 8,000, most copies going to staff members at the 1,730 member institutions, others to the various associate member and subscriber organizations.

The *Business Officer* that appeared in 1977 and after was of thirty-two pages. The magazine's "News" section devoted up to sixteen pages to reports from the Washington-higher education front, other sections—"NACUBO and Regional Association News," "Columns," "Databank"—offering other coverage and short opinion or comment pieces. The magazine absorbed and ended the *Professional File* series, contributions of *File* caliber appearing in a new "Portfolio" section, but with no relaxation of the criteria for their acceptance. (By 1977 the association had published more than eighty-five professional papers in addition to a substantial list of books. Copies of papers in the *Professional File* series would continue to be available on order.) A regular feature was a NACUBO Information Exchange column presenting association responses to institutional questions. The *Professional Calendar* was improved in format, and other columns and features came along. The result was a *Business Officer* that gave its audience each month a single package of information and professional materials, larger but well organized and still modest in design. With Sheppard as contributing editors were, first, Maurese O. Owens, who also was the association librarian, and then other staff members, including Biehl, Wainwright, and Welzenbach, all deeply experienced in serving the association's constituency, and Patti Shafer, a staff associate with Federal Focus and the Energy Task Force.[17]

The Goals and Programs and the Budget and Finance Committees had been busy that year with five-year projections of needs and services—Anthony Lazzaro, vice president, headed the board's Goals and Programs Committee for 1977-78, and Orie Myers, treasurer, the Budget and Finance Committee—and it had become obvious that a dues increase would be necessary. In September 1977, the national board adopted a resolution supporting "in principle" the idea of an increase "no later than June 1, 1979." By January 1978, the board had decided to go ahead immediately with arrangements for the national membership referendum. By May, all had been accomplished. Member institutions approved by a margin of more than two to one—843 to 386—a new schedule that would raise dues payments after June 1, 1978.[18]

Anthony Lazzaro became president in 1978, installed at the annual meeting held July 12-14 in Montreal, a meeting for which the hosts were the Canadian neighbors (the Canadian Association of University Business Officers having been a member of the interassociation group from the beginning) and a meeting that was the first held outside the United States. Serving with Lazzaro were Mary Lai, vice president and president-elect for 1979; Roger Lowe, secretary; and Orie Myers, treasurer. The theme of the meeting was "Flexibility: A Way to Keep Cool in the '80s," and the sessions drew 550 business officers from Canadian and American institutions, including many who attended three "pre-meeting" seminars, new elements in the national scheduling.*

The 1978-79 year was one for moving forward some of the plans shaped by the Goals and Programs Committee and discussed with the board before the dues increase. For a starter, the board approved at its July meeting in Montreal a restructuring of the committee alignment, a move designed, as Lazzaro explained, "to provide for more direct communications between our standing committees and the board." The idea was to effect a more consistent liaison with committees in the field (i.e., those handling major program matters), and the result was an increase in board committees from six to eight—to give a better spread of attention—one of the new committees a merger of the Publications and Professional Development Committees, which were discontinued as separate entities. The board committees thus now were Executive, Bylaws, Budget and Finance, Goals and Programs, Professional Development and Publications, Federal Relations, and Financial and Management Programs. Under the new system each standing committee now reported to one of those committees of the board. To meet the special demands in publications, particularly

---

*The international character of the meeting became evident when certain of the Canadian speakers delivered their papers in French. Simultaneous-translation equipment was installed for the benefit of the U.S. attendees, but the bilingual French-Canadians needed no such help.

with regard to the Administrative Service and the "Portfolio" section of *Business Officer,* the directors created a new Editorial Board (a panel of twenty, widely representative of institutional interests) to review manuscripts and to maintain a broad overview of published and publishable materials.[19]

As the board looked at the future, it was obvious that the area of financial analysis would be growing in importance, for the new problems demanded improvement in the guidelines for handling management information. Scott Hughes had been the association's financial analyst since 1976. Now the board moved not only to give him help but to create what really was a new office. An additional analyst position was authorized in 1978. Early in 1979 Hughes was appointed director of a new Financial Management Center devoted to "improving terminology, definitions, standards, and guidelines" in the field. Soon, to fill the new position, James A. Hyatt (B.A., M.B.A., University of Washington) came to the national staff. Assisting Hughes and Hyatt was Robin Jenkins, financial management intern.[20]

Before the administration changed again, at the national meeting at Atlanta in June 1978, there came shifts in program and staff. On the program front, APPA assumed that spring the major responsibility for direction of the Energy Task Force operations. The move was recommended by the task force itself, since the needs of the institutions had become increasingly technical and passage of the National Energy Conservation Policy Act of 1978 had reduced the need for federal agency liaison, which had been the association's primary role. The internal shifts were occasioned in part by the departure of Richard Biehl, who left the national office to join a private firm, and who was succeeded as director of information and publications by Abbott Wainwright, the veteran of the Administrative Service development. Biehl, the temporary employee of 1971, had worked his way up through the levels of publications activity—a "superb generalist," as Finn described him—and by 1978 he was recognized far beyond the association offices as an expert in certain fields of federal regulation. Not only had he conceived, designed, and launched the looseleaf *Federal Regulations and the Employment Practices of Colleges and Universities,* but he had been solely responsible for the association's HEATH manual, *Guide to Section 504 Evaluation for Colleges and Universities.* But in Wainwright, now the director, the association had a man seasoned by work with *CUBA* and the Administrative Service as with the more general aspects of publications and well known to members of key committees, including Publications and Accounting Principles.[21]

By mid-1979 the association, in another vote by the membership, had amended the national bylaws to permit dues increases to be approved by a majority of the member representatives present and voting at an annual meeting. There would be a thirty-day notice by official publication, but the system would be a simple one (the regional associations had used it for years) and it had the advantage of providing for direct and immediate review and discussion of the needs of the association in its program projections. Simple the system was and, as befit the times, flexible. Member representatives approved it—by mail—926 to 220.[22]

The Atlanta meeting of June 20-22, 1979 brought to the presidency Long Island's Mary Lai, the first woman to hold the office and a financial officer deep in professional experience (as well as in Eastern and National Association activity). To serve with her were Orie Myers, now vice president and the designate for 1980-81, with Roger Lowe continuing as secretary and the new treasurer Robert Carr, of the Office of the Council of State College and University Presidents (State of Washington).

The Atlanta theme was "Management Realities: Today and Tomorrow," and more than 500 business officers were there (some, again, for the new "pre-meeting" seminars). But among all who addressed the difficulties of higher education management in years of stress, it was Clarence Scheps who, speaking of "The Demands of Professionalism," reminded business officers that their obligation was to keep trying forever to improve the management techniques essential to sustain education of the highest quality. And it was time that year, as Scheps undoubtedly believed, to realize what business officer professionals had achieved, in and through their regional and national organizations, as managers in higher education.[23]

The autumn of 1979 marked the twelfth year since the association had opened its national office and the tenth since Francis Finn, having succeeded Kenneth Dick as executive vice president, had moved the office to its new quarters in the National Center for Higher Education. In the decade since 1969, the growth and spread of the association's services were without precedent in higher education. The institutional membership, 980 in 1969, now was 1,873 and still increasing. Where once there had been a scattering of workshops, there now were thirty or more each year ranging from those offering training and retraining in basic techniques to the many dealing with institutional management questions and immediate-action issues of wide concern. Where once had been simply an office, there now was an office containing a widely used and responsive Information Exchange Service, a Federal Focus department dealing with government matters, a Financial Management Center, a circulating library, a main library that contained historical as well as current literature, and the HEARS office that continued to be a central, but not the only, interest of the active Interassociation Management-Related Group. In publications, the diversity of services was unmatched. By 1979 the total national staff included forty-seven persons. As for levels of funding, where total income had been about $250,000 in 1969 (with $140,000 from dues), the total in 1979 was $2,475,000. Membership dues and subscriber fees totaled $970,000, grants and contracts $400,000. Above all, there was a strong relationship with the American Council and other associations and groups with management interests.[24]

A national office organization chart of 1979 showed the allocations of responsibilities by department and director: Information and Publications, Abbott Wainwright; Professional Programs, Sheila Sanjabi; Special Programs, M.J. Williams; Management Programs and Federal Focus, Steven Hychka; Financial Management Center, Scott Hughes; and Business Management, Charles Cochran. The directors and their staff associates were supporting the board and program committees. There had come one committee change, however, that marked in its way the end of a longer period.

Since 1977 there had been discussions within the Committee on Governmental Relations, and between leaders of the committee and the national board, of the committee's evolving role in relation to association sponsorship. The relationship had existed for twenty years—since the days of the federation and George Green's determination to set up a separately supported committee office. But there had arisen a feeling that the committee, functioning in the climate of a new era in federal activity, now needed a more specific identity than it could realize simply as a committee amid an array of committees of the association. The result, finally, was a change in the committee's name and its move, as the *Council* on Governmental Relations, to a separate office on Dupont Circle. The essential link to the association remained, but by December 1979, the committee (now council) had entered, after twenty years, a new phase in its existence.[25]

7

1980 and After

THE 1970s HAD BEEN KNOWN as "the decade of accountability." It was too early, as the 1980s arrived, to see what developments or demands might identify the new era, although certain signs were detectable. While accountability remained a word with a particular meaning to members of the national association, another term was gaining currency too, and this was self-regulation, which referred specifically to a move within higher education to develop its own codes and guidelines as alternatives to federal regulation. The movement was centered in the American Council on Education's Office on Self-Regulation Initiatives, with which the national association was in close contact. When, as 1979 faded, the association chose "Management for Self-Renewal in the 1980s" as the theme of its next annual meeting, the choice seemed revealing. The "self" was there—the idea of self-determination. The theme clearly suggested that the new decade would demand, in colleges and universities, large measures of self-generated administrative discipline.

The impulse toward self-regulation was but one evidence of higher education's need to respond to times in which the signals ranged from mixed to less than heartening. Virtually all institutions were hard-pressed financially and virtually all were feeling the burdens of trying to comply with federal regulations, not alone in the use of federal funds but in areas of equal rights, affirmative action, and equal access for the handicapped. Further, there were disturbing predictions of enrollment decline. A Carnegie Council on Policy Studies in Higher Education was completing in 1980 an extensive report, *Three Thousand Futures: The Next Twenty Years in Higher Education,* forecasting a "golden age" for students—but a "golden age" predicated on a gross enrollment decline of up to 15 percent and a consequent scramble among the institutions in the fields of recruiting, counseling, curriculum adjustment, financing, and placement. The American Council was saying that many institutions, perhaps as many as 600 "less selective liberal arts universities," might not survive to the year 2000. But in the year 1980 the council's self-regulation policy statements were becoming something of an index of contemporary concerns.[1]

The concept of self-regulation had been shaped late in 1978 by an interassociation Task Force on Academic Community Self-Regulation headed by John D. Phillips, president of the National Association of Independent Colleges and Universities. Francis Finn had represented the business officers in the deliberations. Soon the American Council had accepted the task force recommendations and had created, in response, its Office on Self-Regulation Initiatives. The policy statements were not the council's alone, however, but were worked out in each case in cooperation with the higher education associations most directly concerned with the policy issues under examination—and it was a reflection of the times that there now were more than fifty associations representing the various components of the campus community. The very first of the council's policy statements, published in 1979 and setting out guidelines on refunds of student fees, was the result of work by the national association's Student-Related Programs Committee. In succession, thereafter, had come statements on admissions policies, intercollegiate athletics, and management of financial aid, each developed with appropriate interassociation consultations. All of this activity was watched with approval by the U.S. Office of Education, but that office was on its way out. In 1980 there would be a new Department of Education, a thirteenth cabinet-level department that would begin life with a $14.2 billion budget, a staff drawn from half a dozen agencies, and a role—or at least a *raison d'être*—that still needed clarification, especially with regard to its relationship to institutions of higher education.[2]

In such a milieu the national association was advancing familiar projects and testing new ones. The national board having approved a revision of *CUBA*, a steering committee headed by Robert E. Heywood, of Alfred University, soon was preparing for the first complete revision since 1974, with Lanora Welzenbach as editor. The HEARS program, now under a new board of management, was expanding its services and promotional efforts, its circle of sponsoring organizations at twenty. The HEATH project, three years old in 1980, still was commanding cooperative attention. Substantial grants were received for certain major new efforts. Awards of $70,000 came simultaneously from the Exxon Education Foundation and the Lilly Endowment, the first to support a two-year program for the design of a classification model for fund raising and the second to develop a guide for contracting services. The Financial Management Center was at work on a cost accounting handbook for which the Carnegie Corporation of New York had approved by mid-1980 an award of $154,600. A staff change had occurred, meantime, in the Financial Management Center. When Scott Hughes left the office in January 1980 to join a public accounting firm, James Hyatt served as acting director until the permanent position was filled by Stephen D. Campbell, a graduate of Cornell with an M.S. degree in accounting from Virginia, who had served most recently as director of special projects—planning, budgeting, institutional research, personnel administration—in the office of Maryland's vice chancellor of administrative affairs.[3]

Thus work proceeded and changes occurred in the early days of the new decade. But before its annual meeting in St. Louis, the association noted a development that was, in its cumulative way, historic. The institutional membership reached 1,900—1,856 regular members and 44 provisional. There were, in addition, 111 associate members and 175 subscribers. By regional association the distribution was Eastern, 529; Central, 506; Southern, 608; and Western, 257. Thus by 1981 the dues income alone would reach $1,045,000. The association had become, as *Business Officer* modestly put it, "one of the largest higher education groups in the United States." Of that there was no doubt.[4]

The national board of 1980—Long Island's Mary M. Lai still the president—had been instituting examinations in depth of association functions and organizational relationships. For preliminary guidance the board had drafted a paper, "Organization and Delegation of Authority," seeking to clarify the responsibilities of the officers, directors, committees, and staff. At the spring meeting of 1980, held in Washington, D.C., the board made adjustments in this statement, then approved a plan to create a new standing committee on professional development and, with this, the schedule of professional activities for the coming year. But what else the board did seemed a direct response to the times and a confirmation of the direction the new decade was taking. The board adopted a formal resolution urging wide support of the self-regulation objective. The resolution said in part:

> "Self-regulation is a viable concept that needs to be explored to its full potential as an alternative to federally mandated regulations. The current activities of the Office on Self-Regulation Initiatives of the American Council on Education are to be commended. . . . The board hereby resolves that it is committed to the concept of self-regulation and urges all committees of NACUBO and the staff of NACUBO to continue to explore and identify additional potential applications. . . ."

The regional associations also were to be asked to make similar explorations at their institutes and workshops. Not yet could it be said that a "decade of self-regulation" had dawned, but the move toward self-regulation had become, officially, a matter of some urgency.[5]

The year between the national meetings of 1980 and 1981 was a time of analysis and reassessment of national association operations and priorities.

The 1980 meeting—the "Management for Self-Renewal" meeting —was held in June in St. Louis, the main sessions preceded by the pre-meeting seminars, the program oriented to identification of the social and economic pressures to be expected in the 1980s; the principal speakers included Paul C. Reinert, S.J., chancellor of St. Louis University, and Murray L. Weidenbaum, who in 1981 would become chairman of the Council of Economic Advisers in the Reagan Administration. The business officer attendance was about 500.

The president for 1980-81, who had been vice president and president-elect, was Orie Myers, of Emory University, who now succeeded Mary Lai and who carried forward the program-analysis activities with which he already was familiar. A graduate of Emory and an administrator there since 1948, Myers was an experienced hand in professional affairs, once president of CUPA, 1959-60, and later president of the Southern Association, 1974-75, before joining the national board in 1975. Serving with Myers were Roger D. Lowe, Wichita State, vice president; J. Leslie Hicks, Jr., Denison, secretary; and Herman D. Johnson, University of California at San Diego, treasurer. New directors were Robert L. Dan, Black Hawk College; Frederick R. Ford, Purdue; Caspa L. Harris, Jr., Howard; and Fred Vorsanger, Arkansas. Lai remained for the year as director-at-large. The 1980-81 team worked not merely with the new Professional Development Committee, but with an expanded Goals and Programs Committee that was setting its sights on the future.[7]

The fact was that the national association, based firmly on the regionals, had become a higher education management force which had to sort out its primary missions. The association was recognized everywhere, by institutions, by federal agencies, and by other associations, for the quality and scope of its professional services. The fledgling national office to which Francis Finn had come in 1969 now had a staff of forty-seven, an operating budget of $2.6 million, a reserve of $600,000. No association was in higher repute and probably none was turned to more frequently for information or counsel. But the association, as a resource of that character, was frequently pressed, also, to undertake programs that were only marginally within the range of its professional interests or obligations. And the association, no less than its institutions, was facing problems of cost, inflation, use of personnel, and resource management. It was time to identify the main lines. That process was under way.[8]

The 1981 meeting would be held in New York—and at the Waldorf-Astoria, where the first of the annual membership meetings had been held just ten years before—and there would be, perhaps, another of those moments for pointing with pride to the association's growth.* But the 1981 theme would be "Responding to a Changing Environment," and while the association itself prepared to respond, major programs went forward, some to completion, and a new one—a new cooperative program in support of black colleges—was added.

Work at hand that spring of 1981 included the revision of *CUBA*, which was proceeding smoothly, and the fund-raising, contracting, and cost accounting projects supported by Exxon, Lilly, and Carnegie, each of these nearing final form. There also was the HEATH program, on which a final report would be published by summer. But the new program was a long-term addition to the roster of professional commitments. With a grant from the Kellogg Foundation, the United Negro College Fund was sponsoring development of an Integrated Systems Approach (the name thus formalized) to the improvement of management at its forty-one member institutions. The American Council was the primary cooperating agency, but the association would be heavily involved, sharing representation on a management steering committee with the council and the Association of Governing Boards and helping to coordinate the preparation of a systems manual to be assembled with the help of eleven other higher education groups. M.J. Williams would be the association's program monitor and co-manager, but he would be assisted by a new staff member, Mae Hamilton Nash, as the project developed. Nash, with B.S. and M.Ed. degrees from North Carolina A&T and North Carolina at Greensboro, was coming to the association from the Robert R. Moton Memorial Institute, Inc.[9]

When, as the 1981 annual meeting approached, the national directors were advancing their examination of association operations, the results were becoming evident. The board-committee-staff structure now appeared in an organization chart. An ad hoc committee of past presidents was to be available, upon invitation, to consult with the president in office. A policy statement stressed the importance of focusing on professional goals to make certain that new projects, especially sponsored projects, complemented existing efforts. Another encouraged greater use of volunteers and another even closer cooperation with the regional associations. But back of all was a concern about finances in years in which the environment was indeed chang-

---

*The Central Association, at its 1980 annual meeting, pointed with pride to the work of Francis Finn, who had been that association's president when he went to Washington. Finn's services to the profession were cited and he was given, as a memento, a copy of the Frederic Remington bronze, "Bronco Buster."

ing. At a time when the nation's inflation rate was at record highs, the board decided to ask the membership for a modest increase in national dues—an increase proposed reluctantly (the directors acutely aware that institutions were facing their own increased costs), but necessary, as President Myers said, to maintain the association's programs "at their current high level of service." The new schedule, placing more emphasis on institutional expenditure than on enrollment, would be submitted for approval at the meeting in New York. But even though the gross increase in dues income would be only 10 percent (some member institutions actually would be paying less), the directors anticipated a budget deficit in 1981-82. Inflation was a pervasive reality, in the association as on the campus.[10]

The dues increase was approved at the June meeting in New York. Not since creation of the association had such a proposal been rejected, and it was impossible to see in this circumstance anything but a wide and unshakable appreciation—and not by business officers alone—of the association's services. The New York program was a strong one, the "Changing Environment" theme touched first in a keynote address by President Edward J. Bloustein, of Rutgers, and examined from various directions in the subsequent professional sessions. The new president was now Roger Lowe, Orie Myers beginning his year as director-at-large. The vice president and president-elect was Herman Johnson, the secretary Fred Vorsanger, and the treasurer Caspa Harris. New directors were Donald H. Cole, Western Washington University; Donald F. Hume, New York University; and Charles C. Teamer, Dillard University. The new administration had inherited a challenge.[11]

The year had brought changes in certain major staff positions. Charles Cochran, leaving the national office to become the American Council's director of administrative services, was succeeded as business manager by Sheila Sanjabi, the secretary and business office neophyte of 1969 who had handled professional programs since 1970 and who now would be in charge of association business functions. The new director of professional programs was Marie W. Klemann, a graduate of Trinity College and former director of training services for the League of Women Voters. And at the Council on Governmental Relations Reagan Scurlock had retired earlier in the year, his successor Milton Goldberg, who had been assistant executive director for four years. Soon thereafter the new assistant executive director was George B. Bush (B.A., UCLA, M.A., George Washington), who went to the council from Georgetown University, where he had been director of sponsored projects. Scurlock departed with the thanks of the national directors, who noted that the council's roster of participating institutions had been extended from 93 to 123 during his tenure.[12]

Amid developments such as these, the association—its national leadership, its national office, and its more than 1,900 member institutions—moved into the 1980s. Only time could reveal what lay ahead for the national association and the higher education community it served. But certain it was that colleges and universities would need, as never before, informed, alert, and imaginative management. And to serve the institutions best the association would need to preserve the flexibility, the ingenuity, and the willingness to seek solutions that had characterized the years of its rapid growth. The future seemed to be demanding something beyond mere "self-regulation"— perhaps self-development achieved through initiatives reflecting national consensus.*

But if the uncertainties of the future tended sometimes to weigh heavily, the national association itself nevertheless could take satisfaction in what it had become. By 1982, business officers had been in some form of professional affiliation for seventy years, and for longer than that if the first glimmerings of association were considered. They had been organized first by region in 1912 and later, they had come closer together in the federation of 1951, they had formed their national association in 1962, and they had supported a national office since 1967. The periods themselves measured the pace of quickening change in higher education. Yet two characteristics had consistently marked the business officers' approaches to professional tasks. One was a dedication to searching for management principle. From the earliest years, and from the depths of the Great Depression to the tumult of the 1960s and 1970s, business officers had never stopped trying—and *CUBA* was only one of the results—to set out precepts of sound management. The second characteristic, flowing from the first, was a feeling of responsibility to higher education as a whole. Business officers represented only their profession, and through their associa-

---

*The movement toward self-regulation in higher education, originated in 1978, seemed by 1981 peculiarly prescient. The new national administration of President Reagan came to Washington declaring one of its objectives the elimination of unnecessary federal regulations. Soon, Education Secretary Terrel H. Bell, in a talk to the college and university attorneys, said that colleges and universities could indeed look forward to more freedom from federal rules and requirements, and about that time the American Council on Education presented to Vice President Bush, for reference to a White House Task Force on Regulatory Relief, a list of proposed changes in sixty-seven regulations, administered by eighteen federal agencies, that the institutions considered burdensome. Late in the year the decisions still were in suspense, but so too was the future of the new Department of Education, which was being mentioned as one of several departments and offices facing possible elimination or reorientation.

tion they served the small institution and the large, the private and the public, the graduate and the two-year, the established and the emerging. The range was of unprecedented breadth.

From the days of its establishment, the national office had tried in every way to be responsive to professional and institutional needs. It was under Francis Finn that responsiveness became almost explosive. Coming to an office with a small staff, a limited budget, and a national program that still was largely in the "Statement of Aims and Objectives" stage, Finn reached out energetically to move toward the goals then perceived by the national officers and directors. Under the guidance of new committees, workshops were designed and scheduled and manuals for them produced. Information activities were expanded. Contacts were established with other associations and with federal offices. Opportunities for grant support were explored. Major problems, interests, and opportunities for service were identified. The business-related organizations were invited to join what became the Interassociation Management-Related Group. Relationships with the American Council were strengthened. Finn was an energizer, and within a decade the national office had become not merely an association headquarters but a widely used resource—a point of communication, a meeting place, a reference library, a planning center, and an office producing books and other materials that were familiar on most of the campuses of the country. But behind all this were elements of strength that had only needed to be brought together and released. That was the key. The national office represented an association that was based on—that had arisen from—strong regional associations. The association and its office were extensions of the regionals, and business officers themselves, coming from the regionals, were the leaders and molders. Those who served as officers and directors set goals and policies. Those who served with committees shaped the programs. The response was to that constituency at the nearly 2,000 member institutions.

The association seemed to represent, as the 1980s began, a large measure of fulfillment of professional expectations that had been building for a very long time. The elders and pioneers—Arnett, Morey, Hungate, Cain, Erwin, French, Wahlstrom, Stewart, Middlebrook, Van Dyke, many others—had thought as professionals, defining lines of professional activity. When national organization came, activity was released in a flood. Where once there had been few outlets for professional study or writing, both now abounded. Business officers were writing, initiating their own studies, participating in group research. Many were teaching at workshops and many—thousands, in fact—were expanding their horizons as participants in association-sponsored programs. An important result of this expanding emphasis on professional growth was that business officers were being called to serve with, frequently to head, commissions or agencies dealing with higher education affairs. Those who were appointed to the boards or committees of other associations had become, as one observer said, a "glue" that held together, in troubled times, higher education's efforts to deal with complex financial and management problems.

The path had been a long one, that path from 1912 to 1982. Few organizations had been over such a course. But it was to be remembered that few organizations in higher education had begun the walk so early and that there were few with so many members who had done so much, voluntarily, from a simple desire to serve. It was attitude, as much as anything else, perhaps, that identified the professional. The attitude had been there in the beginnings of business officer organizations and it had marked the association's development. The story was in that. But the story also was, at base, the story of people who had great affection for colleges and universities and who came together to try to help preserve the opportunities for learning therein.

Notes

Much of the background information for this history—particularly information on the prefederation and federation years—is drawn, understandably, from the works of C. C. DeLong, the first his *A History of the National Federation of College and University Business Officers Associations* (1963), and the second his unpublished manuscript, "A History of the National Association of College and University Business Officers, 1960-70" (1972), copies of which are in NACUBO archives. Major threads of development are followed thereafter in materials from national and regional association files, including minutes of the national board, transcripts of reports delivered at national or regional meetings, memorandums or correspondence from various sources, and NACUBO publications, primarily the monthly *Business Officer.*

To simplify documentation, sources used most frequently are cited in short forms, DeLong's histories by name and the short title (DeLong, *Federation* or DeLong, *Association*), with page numbers, and board actions by place and date (NACUBO board, Denver, May 3, 1972). Common acronyms of organizations are used (ACE, American Council on Education; CUPA, College and University Personnel Association) when the full name appears in the text. Publications usually appear with full title except where abbreviation is common (*College and University Business Administration, CUBA*).

1   1909-1949: To Build a Base

1. DeLong, *Federation,* pp. 1-3; Preface, *CUBA* (1974), pp. v-vi
2. *Ibid.* (organization of 1912), pp. 3-4
3. Preface, *CUBA* (1974), p. v.
4. DeLong, *Federation,* pp. 6-7
5. *Ibid.,* p. 7; Lloyd Morey, "The Central Association: A Backward Look—A Forward Glance," *Proceedings,* Central Association Golden Anniversary meeting, May 1, 1961
6. Preface, *CUBA* (1974), p. vi
7. DeLong, *Federation,* pp. 7-8
8. Preface, *CUBA* (1974), p. vii
9. *Ibid.,* p. 8; attendance roster, American Association 25th anniversary meeting, Washington, D.C., May 7-8, 1964
10. *Business Officer* (organization of Negro business officers), December 1967
11. DeLong, *Federation,* p. 9
12. Preface, *CUBA* (1974), p. vii

2 1950-1962: The Path to Association

1. Dick, Kenneth A. (notes on regional attitudes), personal communication, February 12, 1981
2. DeLong, *Federation* (Stewart, Middlebrook committees), pp. 38-39; *A Profile: The College and University Interassociation Management Related Group* (organization dates), NACUBO, 1974
3. DeLong, *Federation* (*College and University Business* episode), pp. 10-16
4. *Ibid.* (incorporation, American Council liaison), p. 26
5. *Ibid.* (sixty-college studies), pp. 45-46
6. *Ibid.* (Consulting Service), p. 48; Introduction, *The Sixty College Study—A Second Look, 1957-1958,* National Federation, 1958
7. DeLong, *Federation,* p. 28; Kenneth A. Dick (dues), personal communication
8. *Ibid.,* pp. 41-42
9. *The Committee on Governmental Relations: A Historical Review,* COGR, 1975 (office, Wahlstrom role), pp. 13-14
10. DeLong, *Federation,* pp. 30-31; Kenneth A. Dick, Summary Statement (review), "Proposed Establishment of a National Association of College and University Business Officers," Federation board, February 20, 1961
11. Minutes, National Federation board, Denver, June 23, 1962

3 1963-1969: An Office in Washington

1. DeLong, *Federation* (plan for 1963 assembly), p. 33
2. *Ibid.* (*CUBA* revision), p. 45
3. DeLong, *Federation* (*College and University Business* episode), pp. 10-16
4. DeLong, *Association,* pp. 9, 74-75
5. Committee summary (Kenneth A. Dick, chairman), "Draft of Material as a Guide for Conference of the Committee on Plans for a National Office," April 16, 1965
6. DeLong, *Association,* pp. 10, 77-81
7. *The Committee on Governmental Relations: A Historical Review,* COGR, 1975 (committee in 1965, Wahlstrom's role), pp. 16-17
8. *Ibid.* (Wile), pp. 24-25
9. Minutes, NACUBO board 1967-68, New Orleans, July 19, 1967, Exhibit II: COGR statement, "Principles Concerning Interrelationship Between National Association . . . and Its Committee on Governmental Relations"
10. NACUBO *Newsletter,* Fred S. Vorsanger, editor, June 20, 1967 (Dick appointment), p. 4
11. Minutes, NACUBO board 1967-68, New Orleans, July 19, 1967, Exhibit I: Recommended Budget for the Year 1 June 1967-31 May 1968
12. *Business Officer,* bimonthly series, 1967-68; note on circulation, April 1968
13. *Business Officer* (Small Colleges Committee), April 1968
14. Vorsanger, Fred S., personal communication, January 18, 1982
15. *Business Officer* (American Association gift of funds), September 1968
16. *Ibid.* (pilot workshops on student aid), September 1968, December 1969
17. *Ibid.* (Esso-NACUBO program), December 1967
18. Scheps, Clarence, *"College and University Business Administration—*the 1968 Revision," *Business Officer,* April 1968
19. *The Aims and Objectives of the National Association . . . and a Proposed Timetable for Their Implementation,* September 1968
20. *Business Officer* (bylaws changes), January 1969; (office space, American Council plans), April 1969; (Sanjabi), October 1970
21. *Ibid.* (Dick resignation), November 1968; (Finn selection), June 1969
22. *Ibid.* (national meeting), May, September 1969
23. *Ibid.* (Cain library), May 1969

4 1970-1971: Defining the Professional

1. Morey, Lloyd, "The Central Association: A Backward Look—A Forward Glance," *Proceedings*, Central Association meeting, May 1, 1961
2. *Business Officer* (dues balloting), September 1969, January 1970
3. *Ibid.* (committees), September 1969, August 1970; (WICHE liaison), February 1970
4. *Ibid.* (small college workshops), December 1969, January, November 1970; (senior accounting workshop), March, April 1970
5. *Ibid.* (consultant registry), May 1970; (AACSB), April 1970; (Anderson to staff, then to CUPA), March, September 1970; (Sanjabi to staff associate), October 1970
6. *Ibid.* (special annual report issue 1970-1971), August 1970
7. *Ibid.* *(Professional File)*, February, August 1970
8. *Ibid.* (Accounting Principles Committee), September 1970
9. *Ibid.* (manual revision process), November 1970
10. *Ibid.* (unemployment insurance), November 1970, February 1971; (campus unrest), October 1970; (NACUBO insurance survey), December 1970; (black colleges), November 1970; (affirmative action, employment discrimination), February, June 1971
11. *Ibid.* (national officers, 1971), July 1971
12. *Ibid.* (bylaws amendments), March, April, July 1971; (Community Colleges Committee), March 1971; (insurance projects), December 1970, April 1971
13. *Ibid.* (interassociation talks, HEARS), May, July 1971
14. NACUBO, "Summary of Grants and Contracts, 1969-1979," central files

5 1972-1973: A Time of Proof

1. *Business Officer* (extract texts: Heyns, "The Challenges Are Now," New York; *Chronicle* report of New York meeting), December 1971
2. *Ibid.* (notes on activities), December 1971-January 1973
3. NACUBO, "A Profile of NACUBO: Projections of Growth and Service," 1973
4. *Business Officer* (1972 meeting reports), March-August 1972
5. *Ibid.* (code of ethics), September 1971
6. *Ibid.* (committee lists), August 1971, 1972; NACUBO *Handbooks*, 1971-1972, 1972-1973, 1973-1974
7. *Ibid.* (Hychka), February 1972
8. *Ibid.* *(Professional Calendar)*, June 1972; NACUBO *Studies in Management* series
9. *Ibid.* (Biehl), October 1972; *(Federal Regulations)*, January 1974
10. *Ibid.* (APPA), June 1972; (NACUA), October 1973
11. *Ibid.* (Williams), September 1973; (Information Exchange Service), November 1973
12. *Ibid.* (physical plant management institute), May, August 1972, May 1974; personal notes, 1981, by Steven C. Hychka, NACUBO, and J. Leslie Hicks, Denison
13. *Ibid.* (1973 meeting), April 1973
14. *Ibid.* (Wainwright, Welzenbach), January 1973
15. *Ibid.* (dues increase), April, June, July, October 1973
16. *Ibid.* (AICPA audit guide), April, October 1972, January, September 1973; personal notes, 1981, W. Harold Read
17. *Ibid.* (Administrative Service), February, March, September 1973, January 1974
18. *Ibid.* (accounting research, investment studies), November 1973; (National Commission), December 1973; (Joint Accounting Group), August 1973; (*Risk Management* publication), January 1973
19. *Ibid.* (energy crisis), December 1973
20. *Ibid.* (St. Norbert study, Roger J. Fecher), February 1973; (Florida State study, Don E. Strickland), September 1973; (Purdue study, William Jenkins), November 1973
21. *Ibid.* (Stewart, McElhinney buildings), October 1972; (Baker building), October 1973; (Shea award), May 1974

6 1974-1979: The Theme—Management

1. *Business Officer* (Administrative Service, *CUBA*), January, February 1974
2. Heyns, Roger W., Foreword, *CUBA* (1974)
3. *Business Officer* (Goals and Programs Committee work), February 1974; *(Federal Regulations)*, January, February 1974; *NACUBO Focus* (association income), 1976-77; IMRG (draft *Profile*), agenda, Washington meeting, June 17-18, 1974
4. *NACUBO Focus* (membership growth), 1977-78
5. *Business Officer* (Lowder), April 1977; (HEARS, Cochran, IMRG sponsors), January 1976, January 1978; (Federal Focus, Hychka), February 1976;
   (Hughes), September 1976; (Wainwright, others), November 1976
6. *Ibid.* (Wile), June 1976
7. *Ibid.* (Scurlock)
8. *Ibid.* (Kolinsky, Goldberg), May 1977
9. *Ibid.* (Energy Task Force), February, May 1976, March 1977
10. *Ibid.* (energy manual), April 1977; NACUBO, *Energy Management for Colleges and Universities*, Washington, 1977
11. *Ibid.* (cost reduction program), August, October 1976; (ACE financial status survey), January 1976
12. Internal NACUBO document (project sampling), "Summary of Grants and Contracts, 1969-79"
13. *Business Officer* (administrative leave), March 1976; February, September 1977; February 1978
14. Hunt, Susan, "Nuts-and-Bolts Aid for the Money Men," *Change* magazine, Washington, D.C., April 1976
15. *Business Officer* (Secretariat), January 1976; (HEATH project), *Guide to the Section 504 Self-Evaluation*, January 1978
16. *Ibid.* (APPA move), March 1977; (Cochran as business manager), May 1977; (Lowder resignation), April 1977; (Hunt to HEARS), July 1977
17. *Ibid.* (*Business Officer* to newsmagazine), August, September 1977; other issues of 1978
18. *Ibid.* (dues increase), November 1977; March, June, July 1978
19. *Ibid.* (committee reorganization), September 1978, January 1979
20. *Ibid.* (financial management), June 1979; NACUBO *Focus*, "Financial and Management Programs," 1979-80 *Annual*
21. *Ibid.* (APPA and Energy Task Force), May 1979; (Biehl, Wainwright, staff changes), February 1979
22. *Ibid.* (new dues-increase system), July 1979
23. *Ibid.* (Scheps at 1979 meeting), September 1979
24. *Ibid.* (review of decade), October 1979; NACUBO *Focus*, 1979-80
25. *Ibid.* (from committee to council), December 1979

7 1980 and After

1. *Business Officer* (Carnegie Council report), March 1980
2. *Ibid.* (ACE self-regulation office, activity), August 1978, April, December 1979, February 1980; (Department of Education), December 1979
3. *Ibid.* (*CUBA* revision), December 1979, April 1980; (HEATH progress), January 1980; (Exxon, Lilly awards), April 1980; (cost accounting manual award, Campbell appointment), June 1980
4. *Ibid.* (membership at 1,900), June 1980; (NACUBO dues income, 1981), 1980-81 NACUBO *Annual*
5. *Ibid.* (board meeting, 1980, and resolution on self-regulation), May 1980
6. *Ibid.* (annual meeting, 1980), April, July 1980

7. *Ibid.* (officers, 1980-81, Myers notes), July 1980
8. *Ibid.* (Sanjabi, "Report from the National Office" on NACUBO in 1980), September 1980
9. *Ibid.* (program developments), January, February 1981; (UNCF project), November 1980
10. *Ibid.* (policy and general guidance statements by the national board), May 1981
11. *Ibid.* (national meeting, dues increase approval), September 1981
12. *Ibid.* (Sanjabi to business manager), May 1981; (Klemann to professional programs), August 1981; (Goldberg for Scurlock), December 1980, February 1981; (Bush), April 1981

Appendix A: Organizational Development

Central Association
1912 Organized as Association of Business Officers of the State Universities and Colleges of the Middle West.
1919 "State" dropped from name.
1920 Name changed to Association of University and College Business Officers.
1940 Becomes Central Association of University and College Business Officers.
1946 Becomes Central Association of College and University Business Officers.

Eastern Association
1920 Organized as Association of University and College Business Officers of the Eastern States.
1939 Becomes Eastern Association of College and University Business Officers.

Southern Association
1928 Organized as Southern Association of College and University Business Officers.

Western Association
1936 Organized as Western Association of College and University Business Officers.

American Association
1939 Organized as Association of Business Officers in Schools for Negroes.
1950 Becomes American Association of College and University Business Officers.
1968 Dissolved.

National Federation
1951 Organized as National Federation of College and University Business Officers Associations (regional associations, American Association, National Association of Educational Buyers).
1956 Incorporated.

National Association
1962 Organized as National Association of College and University Business Officers (regional associations, American Association).
1967 Office established in Washington, D.C.
1968 With dissolution of American Association (member institutions joining regionals), organization is national with four regional association components.

Appendix B: National Officers

Federation, 1951-1962

1951-52 *Jamie R. Anthony*, Georgia Tech, president; *James M. Miller*, California, vice president; *Irwin K. French*, Middlebury, secretary-treasurer.

1952-53 *Jamie R. Anthony*, president; *C. C. DeLong*, Illinois, vice president; *Irwin K. French*, secretary-treasurer.

1953-54 *Irwin K. French*, president; *Gerald D. Henderson*, Vanderbilt, vice president; *Nelson A. Wahlstrom*, Washington, secretary-treasurer.

1954-55 *Irwin K. French*, Wellesley, president; *Laurence R. Lunden*, Minnesota, vice president; *Nelson A. Wahlstrom*, secretary-treasurer.

1955-56 *Nelson A. Wahlstrom*, president; *Henry L. Doten*, Maine, vice president; *Charles H. Wheeler III*, Richmond, secretary-treasurer.

1956-57 *Nelson A. Wahlstrom*, president; *Thomas E. Blackwell*, Washington University, vice president; *Charles H. Wheeler III*, secretary-treasurer.

1957-58 *C. O. Emmerich*, Emory, president; *Kurt M. Hertzfeld*, Rochester, vice president; *George W. Green*, Caltech, secretary-treasurer.

1958-59 *C. O. Emmerich*, president; *Kurt M. Hertzfeld*, vice president; *Elmer Jagow*, Knox, secretary; *Wendell G. Morgan*, Howard, treasurer.

1959-60 *Charles H. Wheeler III*, president; *Wilbur K. Pierpont*, Michigan, vice president; *Kenneth A. Dick*, Idaho, secretary; *Wendell G. Morgan,* treasurer.

1960-61 *Charles H. Wheeler III*, president; *Wilbur K. Pierpont*, vice president; *Kenneth A. Dick*, secretary; *Trent C. Root*, Southern Methodist, treasurer.

1961-62 *Wilbur K. Pierpont*, president; *Kenneth A. Dick*, vice president; *Charles E. Prothro*, Tuskegee, secretary; *Trent C. Root*, treasurer.

Association, 1962-1982

1962-63 *Wilbur K. Pierpont*, president; *Kenneth A. Dick*, vice president; *J. W. Bryant*, Hampton, secretary; *Trent C. Root*, treasurer.

1963-65 *Kenneth A. Dick*, president; *Clarence Scheps*, Tulane, vice president; *J. W. Bryant*, secretary; *R. D. Strathmeyer*, Carnegie Tech, treasurer.

1965-66 *Clarence Scheps*, president; *James J. Ritterskamp, Jr.*, Chicago, vice president; *B. A. Little*, Southern, secretary; *R. D. Strathmeyer*, treasurer.

1966-68 *Clarence Scheps*, president; *James J. Ritterskamp, Jr.*, Vassar, vice president; *B. A. Little*, secretary; *W. A. Zimmerman*, Oregon Medical School, treasurer.

1968-69 *James J. Ritterskamp, Jr.*, president; *Kenneth D. Creighton*, Stanford, vice president; *Harold K. Logan*, Tuskegee, secretary; *W. A. Zimmerman*, treasurer.

1969-71   *Kenneth D. Creighton*, president; *Thomas A. McGoey*, Columbia, vice president; *Harold K. Logan*, secretary; *Keith L. Nitcher*, Kansas, treasurer.

1971-72   *Thomas A. McGoey*, president (June-July 1971); *Harold M. Myers*, Drexel, president (July 1971-July 1972); *William T. Haywood*, Mercer, vice president; *Merl M. Huntsinger*, Washington University, secretary; *Glen E. Guttormsen*, San Jose State, treasurer.

1972-73   *William T. Haywood*, president; *Robert W. Meyer*, Ohio Wesleyan, vice president; *Paul W. Hodson*, Utah, secretary; *Lester G. Loomis*, Brandeis, treasurer.

1973-74   *Robert W. Meyer*, president; *Robert B. Gilmore*, Caltech, vice president; *Merrill A. Ewing*, Mount Holyoke, secretary; *Jesse B. Morgan*, Tulane, treasurer.

1974-75   *Robert B. Gilmore*, president; *Merrill A. Ewing*, vice president; *Roger D. Lowe*, Wichita State, secretary; *Jesse B. Morgan*, treasurer.

1975-76   *Merrill A. Ewing*, president; *Jesse B. Morgan*, vice president; *H. S. Thomson*, Washington, secretary; *Donald Marburg*, Minneapolis Society of Fine Arts, treasurer.

1976-77   *Jesse B. Morgan*, president; *Reuben H. Lorenz*, Wisconsin, vice president; *John F. Zeller*, Bucknell, secretary; *A. Dean Buchanan*, California Lutheran, treasurer.

1977-78   *Reuben H. Lorenz*, president; *Anthony D. Lazzaro*, Southern California, vice president; *Mary M. Lai*, Long Island, secretary; *Orie E. Myers, Jr.*, Emory, treasurer.

1978-79   *Anthony D. Lazzaro*, president; *Mary M. Lai*, vice president; *Roger D. Lowe*, secretary; *Orie E. Myers, Jr.*, treasurer.

1979-80   *Mary M. Lai*, president; *Orie E. Myers, Jr.*, vice president; *Roger D. Lowe*, secretary; *Robert L. Carr*, Council of State College and University Presidents (State of Washington), treasurer.

1980-81   *Orie E. Myers, Jr.*, president; *Roger D. Lowe*, vice president; *J. Leslie Hicks, Jr.*, Denison, secretary; *Herman D. Johnson*, California/San Diego, treasurer.

1981-82   *Roger D. Lowe*, president; *Herman D. Johnson*, vice president; *Fred S. Vorsanger*, Arkansas, secretary; *Caspa L. Harris, Jr.*, Howard, treasurer.

Appendix C: Committee Chairpersons

Accounting Principles
1980-82 Stephen H. Terry, Michigan State University
1978-80 David W. Phipps, University of Alabama
1976-78 Harold E. Bell, University of Chicago
1975-76 Reuben H. Lorenz, University of Wisconsin System
1974-75 W. Harold Read, University of Tennessee, and Reuben H. Lorenz, University of Wisconsin System
1972-74 W. Harold Read, University of Tennessee
1970-72 Gilbert L. Lee, Jr., University of Chicago

Council on Governmental Relations (COGR)
1981-82 Kenneth W. Sloan, Ohio State University Research Foundation
1980-81 Joseph S. Warner, Yale University
1979-80 George R. Holcomb, University of North Carolina at Chapel Hill
(Committee on Governmental Relations (COGR))*
1978-79 George R. Holcomb, University of North Carolina at Chapel Hill
1976-78 Robert C. Bowie, The Johns Hopkins University
1975-76 R. L. Anderson, University of Texas System
1973-75 Linda S. Wilson, Washington University and University of Illinois
1971-73 Norman H. Gross, University of California System
1970-71 Clinton T. Johnson, University of Minnesota
1969-70 Robert F. Kerley, The Johns Hopkins University
1967-69 Ernest M. Conrad, University of Washington
1965-67 Lytle J. Freehafer, Purdue University

(The committee began in 1948; this list dates only to establishment of the NACUBO office.)

Energy Task Force
1981-82 H. Val Peterson, Utah State University
1980-81 Lawrence L. Landry, Swarthmore College
1979-80 Joe L. Estill, Jr., Duke University
1977-79 Daniel J. Altobello, Georgetown University
1975-77 John F. Embersits, Yale University

Facilities Planning and Management
1980-82 William L. Erickson, San Diego State University
1978-80 Walter L. Pike, Dallas County Community College District
1976-78 Daniel J. Altobello, Georgetown University
1974-76 Elmo R. Morgan, University of California-Berkeley

*Indicates earlier name of committee.

(Facilities)*
1972-74   Charles E. Diehl, George Washington University
(Facility Construction)*
1971-72   Harry E. Brakebill, California State Colleges
(Facility Construction and College Housing)*
1970-71   Harry E. Brakebill, California State Colleges
1969-70   Elmo R. Morgan, University of California-Berkeley
1969   Robert F. Kerley, The Johns Hopkins University

Financial Management
1981-82   William E. Vandament, Ohio State University and New York
            University
1979-81   Robert K. Thompson, University of Washington
1979-80   William R. Odom, Department of Education, State of Florida
(Costing Standards)*
1978-79   Allan W. Barber, University of Georgia
1977-78   Frederick R. Ford, Purdue University
1974-77   John L. Green, Jr., Rensselaer Polytechnic Institute and University
            of Miami
(Cost Studies)*
1973-74   John L. Green, Jr., Rensselaer Polytechnic Institute
1969-73   Loren M. Furtado, University of California-Berkeley
1969   Keith L. Nitcher, University of Kansas

Insurance and Risk Management
1981-82   Claudina Madsen, Foothill-De Anza Community College District
1980-81   Joe F. Evans, Washington University
1978-80   Ronald E. Sapp, The Johns Hopkins University
1976-78   John F. Adams, Georgia State University
1974-76   Warren R. Madden, Iowa State University
1973-74   Anthony D. Lazzaro, University of Southern California
(Insurance)*
1970-73   David R. Baldwin, Wayne State University and Temple University

Investments
1975-82   Rodney H. Adams, Stanford University
1972-75   John M. Dozier, Macalester College and Kalamazoo College
1971-72   G. C. Henricksen, Duke University
1968-71   John F. Meck, Dartmouth College

Manual Revision
1969-73   Robert B. Gilmore, California Institute of Technology

Membership
1974-75   Dennis Blossom, University of Missouri
1973-74   Merrill A. Ewing, Mount Holyoke College

*Indicates earlier name of committee.

101

1972-73   Jesse B. Morgan, Tulane University
1971-72   Lester G. Loomis, Brandeis University
1969-71   Harold M. Myers, Drexel University

Minority Institutions
1981-82   D. L. Brooks, Jarvis Christian College
1979-81   William T. Shropshire, Huston-Tillotson College
1977-79   Harold A. Jenkins, South Carolina State College
1976-77   Curtis Holt, Jr., Benedict College
(Management at Black Colleges)*
1974-76   Caspa L. Harris, Jr., Howard University
1973-74   Harvey R. Alexander, Johnson C. Smith University
1972-73   A. L. Palmer, Howard University
1971-72   Bernie A. Little, Southern University, and A. L. Palmer, Howard University

Personnel
1980-82   Lee A. Ellis, Northwestern University
1979-80   Joseph C. O'Connell, Rutgers, The State University
1977-79   Gene M. Nordby, Georgia Institute of Technology
1976-77   Stanford R. Bohne, University of Tennessee
1975-76   Robert F. Kerley, University of California-Berkeley
1974-75   John F. Embersits, Yale University
1972-74   Carl A. Kasten, Drake University
1971-72   Mary M. Lai, Long Island University
1969-71   Orie E. Myers, Jr., Emory University
1968-69   Thomas A. McGoey, Columbia University

Postal Regulations and Service
1980-82   Harold R. Bland, Roosevelt University
1978-80   Merrill A. Ewing, Mount Holyoke College
1976-78   Joe Winegar, Texas Tech University
(ad hoc committee from 1973 to 1976)

Professional Development
1980-82   Frederick R. Ford, Purdue University
1978-80   (no committee)
1975-78   James R. Buchholz, Rochester Institute of Technology and University of Missouri
1973-75   Fred S. Vorsanger, University of Arkansas
1971-73   Frederick R. Ford, Purdue University
1969-71   Clarence Scheps, Tulane University

Programs for Small Colleges
1981-82   Paul J. Aslanian, Macalester College
1977-81   Thomas O. James, Chatham College and Birmingham Southern College

*Indicates earlier name of committee.

1975-77   J. Leslie Hicks, Jr., Denison University
1973-75   A. Dean Buchanan, California Lutheran College
1971-73   Marwin O. Wrolstad, Lawrence University
1968-71   William T. Haywood, Mercer University

Publications
1976-78   Robert L. Carr, Office of the Council of State College and University Presidents (State of Washington)
1973-76   Kurt M. Hertzfeld, Amherst College
1969-73   Vincent Shea, University of Virginia
1969   W. A. Zimmerman, University of Oregon Medical School

Resource Planning and Management
1973-75   Clarence Scheps, Tulane University

Student-Related Programs
1981-82   Lester Brookner, Miami-Dade Community College
1978-81   Gerald M. Skogley, University of North Dakota
1976-78   Kenneth W. Heikes, Eastern Montana College
(Student Aid)*
1975-76   Kenneth W. Heikes, Eastern Montana College
1974-75   William H. McMillion, West Virginia University, and Frank I. Wright, Carleton College
1973-74   William H. McMillion, West Virginia University
1969-73   Lloyd A. Keisler, Indiana University
1969   Luther C. Callahan, University of Alabama

Taxation
1979-82   John A. Falcone, Lafayette College
1977-79   John W. Woltjen, Lehigh University
1975-77   Robert E. Heywood, Alfred University
1973-75   Merl M. Huntsinger, Washington University
1972-73   Douglass Hunt, Columbia University
1971-72   John E. Ecklund, Yale University
1968-71   Donald E. Blanchard, Knox College

Two-Year Colleges
1979-82   W. L. Prather, Amarillo College
1977-79   Jim B. Bolin, Westark Community College
1976-77   Myron G. Talman, Junior College District of Metropolitan Kansas City, Missouri
1975-75   David E. Hilquist, Oakton Community College
1973-75   John C. Robertson, Junior College District of St. Louis
1972-73   William B. Cutler, Foothill-De Anza Community College District
(Community Colleges)*
1971-72   William B. Cutler, Foothill-De Anza Community College District

*Indicates earlier name of committee.

Appendix D: Presidents of Regional Associations

Central Association

1912-14	Shirley W. Smith
1914-16	Carl E. Steeb
1916-18	George H. Hayes
1918-19	H. J. Thorkelson
1919	M. E. McCaffrey
1919-20	Trevor Arnett
1920-21	U. H. Smith
1921-22	Lloyd Morey
1922-23	J. C. Christensen
1923-24	A. J. Lobb
1924-25	J. D. Phillips
1925-26	Edward E. Brown
1926-27	W. T. Middlebrook
1927-28	W. H. Bates
1928-29	Herman Knapp
1929-30	R. B. Stewart
1930-31	F. H. Walcott
1931-32	D. H. Peak
1932-33	T. C. Carlson
1933-34	H. H. Halladay
1934-35	F. E. Smith
1935-36	L. E. Gunderson
1936-37	Charles A. Kuntz
1937-38	Ralph J. Watts
1938-39	Karl Klooz
1939-40	Harry Wells
1940-42	William H. Cobb
1942-44	J. L. Lindsey
1944-46	A. W. Peterson
1946-47	C. D. Simmons
1947-48	T. E. Blackwell
1948-49	Herbert Watkins
1949-50	F. W. Ambrose
1950-51	John K. Selleck
1951-52	Laurence R. Lunden
1952-53	Bruce Pollock
1953-54	Jacob Taylor
1954-56	C. C. DeLong

1956-57	Roscoe Cate
1957-58	J. Parker Hall
1958-59	Robert W. Hoefer
1959-61	Harlan S. Kirk
1961-62	Ralph Olmsted
1962-63	G. E. Harwood
1963-64	C. F. McElhinney
1964-66	James J. Ritterskamp, Jr.
1966-67	Joseph A. Franklin
1967-68	Keith L. Nitcher
1968-69	Robert W. Meyer
1969	D. Francis Finn
1969-70	Merl M. Huntsinger
1970-71	Lloyd Goggin
1971-72	Richard G. Vogel
1972-73	Donald Marburg
1973-74	Ray H. Bezoni
1974-75	Reuben H. Lorenz
1975-76	Harlan E. Cain
1976-77	John M. Dozier
1977-78	Roger D. Lowe
1978-79	Walter R. Jahn
1979-80	Frederick R. Ford
1980-81	Warren R. Madden
1981-82	Joe F. Evans

Eastern Association

1920-21	C. S. Danielson
1921-22	W. O. Miller
1922-23	G. C. Wintringer
1923-24	E. A. Burlingame
1924-25	C. D. Bostwick
1925-26	F. B. Johnson
1926-27	H. C. Edgerton
1927-28	R. N. Ball
1928-29	E. B. Earnshaw
1929-30	L. E. Kimball
1930-31	H. S. Ford
1931-32	E. I. Carruthers

1932-33	G. F. Sheers	

Southern Association

1932-33	G. F. Sheers
1933-34	A. G. Wilkinson
1934-35	G. F. Rogalsky
1935-36	A. S. Johnson
1936-37	George P. Hyde
1937-38	B. W. Tabb
1938-39	G. S. Rupp
1939-40	G. D. Crofts
1940-41	Raymond L. Thompson
1941-42	Frank L. Jackson
1942-43	Gail A. Mills
1943-44	Lester L. Lapham
1944-45	W. Emerson Gentzler
1945-46	W. R. Wagenseller
1946-47	R. C. Magrath
1947-48	Henry W. Herzog
1948-49	Boardman Bump
1949-50	H. R. Patton
1950-51	D. L. Rhind
1951-52	C. H. Wheeler III
1952-53	F. Morris Cochran
1953-54	John W. S. Littlefield
1954-55	W. R. Hendershot
1955-56	Marcus Robbins
1956-57	John Schlegel
1957-58	Edward K. Cratsley
1958-59	John F. Meck
1959-60	Vincent Shea
1960-61	Richard D. Strathmeyer
1961-62	Charles C. Pyne
1962	Kenneth R. Erfft
1962-63	Kenneth J. Plant
1963-64	Wilbur M. Young
1964-65	Bruce J. Partridge
1965-66	Kurt M. Hertzfeld
1966-67	Thomas A. McGoey
1967-68	Harold M. Myers
1968-69	Lester G. Loomis
1969-70	Ross Ellis
1970-71	Merrill A. Ewing
1971-72	Paul R. Linfield
1972-73	Norman W. Myers
1973-74	Frank R. Stone
1974-75	Mary M. Lai
1975-76	Anthony T. Procelli
1976-77	J. Leslie Hicks, Jr.
1977-78	George B. May
1978-79	Caspa L. Harris, Jr.
1979-80	Donald F. Hume
1980-81	Raymond M. Krehel
1981-82	Alvin N. Ward

Southern Association

1928-29	G. H. Mew
1929-30	S. W. Garrett
1930-33	N. M. Yielding
1933-34	K. H. Graham
1934-35	F. L. Jackson
1935-36	Thurman Sensing
1936-37	J. C. Kellum
1937-38	Rupert Cook
1938-39	E. T. Brown
1939-40	R. B. Cunningham
1940-41	A. M. Graham
1941-42	W. C. Turner
1942-43	Gerald D. Henderson
1943-44	H. A. Meyer
1944-46	S. F. Bretske
1946-47	W. Wilson Noyes
1947-48	G. R. Kavanaugh
1948-49	W. T. Ingram
1949-50	C. B. Markham
1950-51	J. R. Anthony
1951-52	Gladys Barger
1952-53	Frank D. Peterson
1953-54	J. H. Dewberry
1954-55	C. O. Emmerich
1955	G. F. Baughman
1955-56	W. M. Murphy
1956-57	R. K. Shaw
1957-58	C. M. Reaves, Jr.
1958-59	G. C. Hendricksen
1959-60	Clarence Scheps
1960-61	C. L. Springfield
1961-62	Trent C. Root
1962-63	J. G. Vann
1963-64	Eugene E. Cohen
1964-65	Luther C. Callahan
1965-66	V. Howard Belcher
1966-67	W. Clyde Freeman
1967-68	J. F. Bosch, Jr.
1968-69	William T. Haywood
1969-70	Dud Giesentanner
1970-71	W. Harold Read
1971-72	Jesse B. Morgan
1972-73	A. J. Osborne
1973-74	Orie E. Myers, Jr.
1974-75	E. E. Davidson
1975-76	Harold K. Logan
1976-77	Edwin G. Beggs
1977-78	James H. Colvin
1978-79	Lee A. Barclay, Sr.
1979-80	Fred S. Vorsanger

105

1980-81	Charles C. Teamer
1981-82	John L. Temple

Western Association

1937	E. S. Erwin
1938	H. A. Bork
1939	H. H. Benedict
1940	Fred F. McLain
1941	Charles A. Robbins
1942	E. S. Thompson
1945	O. D. Garrison
1946	J. Orville Lindstrom
1947	William J. Norton
1948	Paul A. Walgren
1949-50	Alf E. Brandin
1950-51	Elton D. Phillips
1951-52	Nelson A. Wahlstrom
1952-53	Robert W. Fenix
1953-54	George W. Green
1954-55	James M. Miller
1955-56	Gerald Banks
1956-57	Glen C. Turner
1957-58	Kenneth A. Dick

1958-59	Duncan I. McFadden
1959-60	Ernest M. Conrad
1960-61	Harry E. Brakebill
1961-62	Robert B. Gilmore
1962-63	William A. Zimmerman
1963-64	H. S. Thomson
1964-65	Dwight Adams
1965-66	Donald Nelson
1966-67	Gurnett Steinhauer
1967-68	Paul W. Hodson
1968-69	Bo-Wilhelm Skarstedt
1969-70	Janet B. Hoit
1970-71	J. W. Watts
1971-72	Anthony D. Lazzaro
1972-73	Robert R. Winterberg
1973-74	Walter N. McLaughlin
1974-75	William B. Cutler
1975-76	Herman D. Johnson
1976-77	Robert L. Carr
1977-78	Glen E. Guttormsen
1978-79	A. Dean Buchanan
1979-80	Philip L. Davis
1980-81	Donald H. Cole
1981-82	Carroll J. Lee

Appendix E: Contributors

Carnegie Corporation of New York
Equitable Life Assurance Society of the United States (unrestricted)
Exxon Corporation
Exxon Education Foundation
Ford Foundation
General Motors Corporation
IBM Corporation
Lilly Endowment, Inc.
United States Steel Foundation, Inc.
W. K. Kellogg Foundation

Contributors to the Comparative Performance Study
David L. Babson & Co., Inc.
A. G. Becker Incorporated
John W. Bristol & Co.
Continental Illinois National Bank and Trust Company of Chicago
Fayez Sarofim & Co.
Hartford National Bank and Trust Company
Loomis Sayles & Company
Merrill Lynch Asset Management, Inc.
T. Rowe Price Associates, Inc.
Provident National Bank
Salomon Brothers
State Street Bank and Trust Company
Thorndike, Doran, Paine & Lewis

Appendix F: Long-Service Employees

The following list contains the names of former employees who had at least five years of service and employees who had at least five years of service as of April 30, 1982.

Former Employees

G. Richard Biehl
Charles M. Cochran, Jr.
Peter A. Hickey
Neal O. Hines
Dorothy Kolinsky
Howard P. Wile

Employees as of April 30, 1982

D. F. Finn
Milton Goldberg
Steven C. Hychka
Michael P. Marrone
Genevieve T. McMahon
Maurese O. Owens
Sheila R. Sanjabi
Jeffrey M. Sheppard
Abbott Wainwright
Michael Weaver
Lanora Welzenbach
M. J. Williams
Roma H. Zimmer

Appendix G: NACUBO Mission and Goals

Mission

NACUBO's mission is to promote sound management and financial administration of colleges and universities and to anticipate the issues affecting higher education.

Goals

- To represent colleges and universities by:

  reflecting management and financial interests of higher education at the national level;

  serving as an information resource on management and financial administration in higher education;

  providing leadership in activities related to the principles and practices on which management and financial administration are based;

  projecting to the federal government the issues of concern to higher education to the extent that government programs affect management and financial administration.

- To foster cooperation with and among the regional associations.

- To provide opportunities for basic and advanced training, career development, skill improvement, and other forms of professional growth in management and financial administration in higher education.

- To gather information that will assist in the management and financial administration of colleges and universities, and to stimulate research and the development of sound practices in these fields.

- To disseminate information related to the management and financial administration of colleges and universities by providing information:

  that relates to the principles on which management and financial administration are based;

  that is of a practical nature and assists in day-to-day institutional operations;

  that increases awareness of current issues in higher education;

  that reports on results of research and efforts to develop sound practices in these fields.

- To encourage cooperation with organizations having common interests in management and financial administration of higher education.

- To promote and maintain professional standards and ethical conduct for management and financial administrators of higher education.

109

Index